You're Too
Smart for This

(Beating the 100 Big Lies about
Your First Job)

Michael Ball

SOURCEBOOKS, INC.®
NAPERVILLE, ILLINOIS

Published by Sourcebooks, Inc.
P.O. Box 4410, Naperville, Illinois 60567-4410
(630) 961-2168
Fax: (630) 961-2168
www.sourcebooks.com

Library of Congress Cataloging-in-Publication Data

Ball, Michael
  You're too smart for this : beating the 100 big lies about your first job / Michael Ball.
      p. cm.
  ISBN-13: 978-1-4022-0598-9
  ISBN-10: 1-4022-0598-8
  1. Vocational guidance. 2. Career development. 3. College graduates—Vocational guidance. 4. College graduates—Employment. 5. Office politics. 6. Work environment. I. Title: You are too smart for this. II. Title.

HF5381.B242 2006
650.1—dc22

                                                      2005025118

Printed and bound in the United States of America.
VP 10 9 8 7 6 5 4 3 2 1

For Evie, until I get married. Or serious.

Contents

Introduction: What, You Actually Bought That? 1

    Lie no. 1: You're Going to Love Your First Couple
        of Jobs 2

Chapter no. 1: School Lied to You First 9

    Lie no. 2: College Taught You How to Function
        Off-Campus 10

    Lie no. 3: You're Too Young for an Identity
        Crisis 13

    Lie no. 4: Work Is Going to Challenge You Like Your
        Classes Did 16

    Lie no. 5: You Can Expect Similar Performance
        Feedback 19

Chapter no. 2: You're Too Smart for This 23

    Lie no. 6: Your College Degree Actually Means
        Something 24

    Lie no. 7: If You Got Hired, It Means They Trust You ...27

    Lie no. 8: You'll Be Doing the Job That the Company
        Described 30

    Lie no. 9: You're Too Smart for This 33

    Lie no. 10: Intelligence Makes Up for Experience 36

    Lie no. 11: You Can at Least Bitch about Your
        Gruntwork 39

    Lie no. 12: Do Whatever Is Asked of You 41

Chapter no. 3: Misconceptions about Managers, Coworkers,
and Others Who Regularly Piss You Off . .45

Lie no. 13: You Don't Have to Manage Your
Manager 46

Lie no. 14: Your Boss Knows How Your Projects Are
Going 50

Lie no. 15: Managers Just Love Surprises 53

Lie no. 16: It's More Important to Be Smart Than to
Be Liked 56

Lie no. 17: Individual Performance Comes Before
Teamwork 59

Lie no. 18: Go Ahead, Flaunt Your Success 62

Lie no. 19: You Can Handle It Without a Mentor 65

Lie no. 20: Your Mentor Is Your New Best
Friend 69

Lie no. 21: Don't Disturb the Veterans in the Office 72

Lie no. 22: Networks Are for More Established
Professionals 75

Chapter no. 4: The Daily Grunt 79

Lie no. 23: You Can Still Turn in a "B"
Assignment 80

Lie no. 24: If You're Good, You Shouldn't Make
Mistakes 83

Lie no. 25: Try to Downplay Your Screw-Ups 87

Lie no. 26: People Remember What They Said, Asked, or
Promised 91

Lie no. 27: Colleagues Should Know How Long Things
Take You 94

Lie no. 28: If You Don't Know, Guess 97

Lie no. 29: You Can Lie, Cheat, and Steal Like in
College 101

Lie no. 30: You Still Need a Professor to
Teach You 105

Lie no. 31: No Need to Learn the Business If You Do Your
Job Well 108

Lie no. 32: Reading and Classes Were Only
for School 111

Chapter no. 5: Branding Your Grunt 115

Lie no. 33: You're One-of-a-Kind to the Company 116

Lie no. 34: Just Blend in with the Crowd 119

Lie no. 35: Try to Do Everything Well 122

Lie no. 36: People Already Know What You Can Do for
Them 125

Lie no. 37: You'll Get Remembered Just by
Being There 128

Lie no. 38: Be Known for Many Things 131

Lie no. 39: Your Brand Can Stand on Its Own 134

Lie no. 40: Brands Take Care of Themselves 137

Chapter no. 6: Lies, Damn Lies, and Office
Politics 141

Lie no. 41: The Company Works How It Says
It Does 142

Lie no. 42: Feel Free to Voice Your Concern 145

Lie no. 43: You Can Play Politics Once You Understand
Them 148

Lie no. 44: To Get What You Want, Do What You
Have To 151

Lie no. 45: Downtime Is Your Own Time 154

Lie no. 46: You've Got the Best Ideas 157

Lie no. 47: Good Ideas Sell Themselves 160

Lie no. 48: Politics Don't Affect Good Ideas 163

Lie no. 49: Ideas Are as Good When Coming

from You 166

Lie no. 50: You Can Sleep with Your Coworkers 169

Chapter no. 7: It's Up or Out 173

Lie no. 51: Promotions Are Based on Hard Work 174

Lie no. 52: Colleagues Don't Influence

Promotions 177

Lie no. 53: You'll Get Promoted During a Bad

Stretch 180

Lie no. 54: The Job Has to Exist for You to

Get It 183

Lie no. 55: Transfers Aren't as Good as

Promotions 186

Lie no. 56: Politically, Transfers Are No Problem 189

Lie no. 57: Up Is the Only Way Out 192

Chapter no. 8: Finding Your Work - Lie Balance 195

Lie no. 58: The Company Cares about Your

Outside Life 196

Lie no. 59: You Have to Work Harder at the Beginning .199

Lie no. 60: More Hours, More Success 202

Lie no. 61: Burnout Only Happens to Older Workers . . .205

Lie no. 62: The Job Should Dictate Your Priorities 208

Lie no. 63: No Time for Balance .211

Lie no. 64: You Can't Say No 214

Lie no. 65: Your Love Life Comes Later 217

Lie no. 66: You'll Find "The One" in a Bar 220

Lie no. 67: Online Dating Is the Answer 223

Lie no. 68: You Can Rest When You're Dead 226

Chapter no. 9: Do What You Love, and You'll
                    Probably Starve 229

Lie no. 69: Most Careers Are Carefully Chosen 230

Lie no. 70: People Know Where They're Going
                    Professionally 233

Lie no. 71: Values Generally Guide Work 236

Lie no. 72: Jobs Are Often Fulfilling and
                    Enjoyable 239

Lie no. 73: Work Is about Money, Not Purpose 242

Lie no. 74: Do What You Love, and You'll Probably
                    Starve................................245

Lie no. 75: Passions Are Always End-All, Be-All 248

Chapter no. 10: The Money Will Make You Happy 251

Lie no. 76: The Money Will Make You Happy 252

Lie no. 77: Cash Now, Dreams Later 255

Lie no. 78: Executives Are Really Important People 258

Lie no. 79: Money Says a Lot about You 261

Lie no. 80: You Can Have It All 264

Lie no. 81: The Safe Move Is a Safe Move 267

Lie no. 82: You'll Wish You Spent More Time at
                    the Office 270

Chapter no. 11: Don't Worry, the Company Will Take Care
                    of You 273

Lie no. 83: There's Still a Ladder to Climb 274

Lie no. 84: You've Got a Résumé to Worry About 277

Lie no. 85: You Only Get One Career 280

Lie no. 86: The Company Will Keep You During Lean
Times 283

Lie no. 87: Getting Laid-Off Is a Big Deal 286

Lie no. 88: Put Your Identity into Your Job 289

Lie no. 89: Get Close to Your Coworkers 292

Lie no. 90: Quit When It Gets Bad 295

Chapter no. 12: What's Wrong with What's Next 299

Lie no. 91: You Should Know What's Next 300

Lie no. 92: Get Excited, Not Stressed 303

Lie no. 93: Everything Will Go According to Plan 306

Lie no. 94: Trial and Error Is a Bad Thing 309

Lie no. 95: Knowing What You Should Do Means
Doing It 312

Lie no. 96: It's All Going to Happen Fast 315

Lie no. 97: Failure Means You're Wrong or Not Good
Enough 318

Lie no. 98: Success Is More Talent Than Hard Work 321

Lie no. 99: They're Behind You All the Way 324

Lie no. 100: Irrational Is Impossible 327

Acknowledgments 331

About the Author 333

Index 335

What, You Actually Bought That?

> Come now! ...Were everything clear, all would seem to you vain.

—Marcel Proust, French author who reminds us that half the fun is in undressing each other

Lie no. 1
You're Going to Love Your First Couple of Jobs

First off, congrats on graduating (or almost), as well as on your post-college sobriety (or almost) as you thumb through this book. Not that you don't have every opportunity to play hide-and-go-seek with alcoholism again at the entry level. It's just that four, five, or—my favorite—six years is a really long time to mess with your liver like that when it's not out of anger or depression. At least in Corporate America your drinking is much more justifiable, and sometimes even expensed to the firm.

Which isn't to say that your other cube will be at the bar, necessarily, but starting off in your career is actually pretty close to losing your virginity: A little rushed, sometimes painful, not who you thought it'd be with, kind of awkward, and altogether short of what it was built up to be. The main difference, I suppose, is that the entry level lasts way longer than you ever

> " Any fool can tell the truth, but it requires a man of some sense to know how to lie well. "
>
> —English novelist Samuel Butler, who was a sheep rancher for four years, and who had sense enough to lie about how he kept warm at night

did, and seldom asks you what you're thinking about, because you seem so distant.

Although that still doesn't mean you shouldn't do it, naturally, because it only gets better and sexier and more fun—especially once you find the right partner. And like you really have a choice at this point but to hold hands with some company that's going to pick up your health insurance premium, because would you care to tell me what else you intend to do with your shiny new poli-sci degree? I know your educational lenders are certainly curious.

But let's back up for a minute; it's this kind of thinking that got our parents in trouble and led to polyester suits. What's really been accomplished so far? You were able to fabricate a résumé of things you would've liked to have done, ideally, and then unloaded your undergrad story on a handful of half-cocked mid-tier managers. Great, you're well on your way toward paying rent on time, and realizing your true potential for dissatisfaction, just like your friends who went into banking and consulting.

No, there's got to be more to it than that: a vision, a purpose, a *raison d'etre* (French for not making it up as you go along). Plus who do you think did the better

> " Work is uninspiring, unappreciated, and underpaid—unless you're out of it. "
>
> —Robert Half, who founded a big temp agency to prove his point

snow job—you, or the people who do this to buy their kids braces and take vacations in Colorado? Not to discount your flair for salesmanship, but they doubtlessly saw right past your bullshit long before you ever concocted the nonsense scenario you used to answer the "Tell me about a time you had to deal with conflict in a group setting..." question. Your brand probably just smelled the least bad out of everyone else's.

Which is when you come to find out that the corporate entry level is, in fact, a silly and wasteful culture of gruntwork, brownnosing, and near-slips into a coma. So whatever you were whispered in secrecy by anyone wearing a polo shirt with a company logo embroidered on it (e.g., "You know, just between you and me, you're our favorite candidate, and let me tell you again about our 'flextime' program..."), forget it. It was a line to get you into bed. And who knew you were that easy?

No, there's a way to play this where you're both going to need a cigarette afterward. See, when you put up with the crap that gets shoveled onto your desk, and patiently milk the company for knowledge, experience, and professional direction, you can then go put that toward a career you're passionate about—one you love

Brave New Slacker

"Like every man of sense and good feeling, I abominate work."

—Aldous Huxley

and actually want to call the next day to talk about what a great time you had last night.

But you can't expect that right away, of course. Finding what you were made to do is the task of a lifetime (quite literally), and you can't possibly know yourself or the world well enough during your first few years out of school to make any kind of reasonable determination. Instead, you've got to hang out for a while, see what's up out here, figure out what blows your hair back versus what just blows.

And, again, for all the idiocy and ass-backwardness of the corporate workplace, it's a hell of an education (now that you're done, officially, being educated). In a lot of ways, you're getting paid to learn now, albeit in a place you don't really want to be—which is such an interesting twist from going into massive debt to not learn in a place you wish you would've never left. (Yeah, read it again.)

Oh, Sorry, I'm Just Here for the Money

- A 2004 Associated Press poll found that young adults eighteen to twenty-nine were most likely to say their job was something they do mainly to earn a paycheck.

- People over thirty were much more likely to express satisfaction with their work.

- Nobody polled liked sitting in a cube.

Well, in any case, no turning back now, so let's get on board with things, shall we? Some issues you'll be able to fix, most you won't. That's what the bulk of this book is about—to help you tell the difference, and explain how to position yourself accordingly. The rest is to shine a light on that dark little corner where you've carelessly dumped your values, and to see if you can't, I don't know, uncover your calling and realize your greater purpose for existing on this planet. Or whatever.

Heady and ambitious? Of course it is. But if you don't start thinking about this stuff now, it's only going to get harder as you get deeper into it—like that person you were never really into, but just kept dating, and now look at you.

> **Most people would sooner die than think; in fact, they do so.**
>
> —Bertrand Russell, British philosopher, mathematician, and Nobel laureate who probably did enough thinking for all of us

So big ups again on finishing school, and on beating out everyone else to land this gig; they have every reason not to like you, and you should drink that in. Still, it's just a temp job, whatever you want to call it (I'll give you a year or two, generously), meaning you need to keep all this in perspective.

No matter how badly things go, or who you piss off, or what you get caught doing in the Xerox room, it's all going to go away sooner rather than later. And then you get to dig your hole again, except this time hopefully enjoying your screwups more, and pissing people off who you like much better.

But it'll even suck then at times, so I'd better not see this copy sitting used on Amazon.com for $4.99. You're just going to end up buying it back, but from someone who's highlighted the parts you already know. Besides, you'll forget the quotes and anecdotes, and I didn't spend all that time digging through old books to have you butcher this stuff when you're trying to pass off my advice as your own.

Which, by the way, I'm very impressed with. Keep it up, you'll be a great manager in no time.

1

School Lied to You First

Lie no. 2
College Taught You How to Function Off-Campus

Hitting the workforce is a lot like hitting puberty again: Suddenly you're gawky, unsure of how to carry yourself, arguing with new feelings, and still dropping $8 a bottle on Clearasil. In any event, your voice is bound to crack as you come of age in the office—dropped off from college, precisely, neither here nor there. Part student, part grunt, you're the bastard love child of the liberal arts and its dirty mistress, reality.

Some say that our academic community is sitting around the ivory tower in a big intellectual circle-jerk; others think they're impractical on purpose—that they've got an axe to grind with the professionals screwing with their theories and pulling in a quarter mil a year. Either way, there's only so much you can do with Shakespeare and Plato when you've got a client who's lost it with you. Thinking back to something useful, all I can recall is that my

> " **A man becomes a creature of his uniform.** "
>
> —Napoleon Bonaparte, whose left hand really told the story here

sociology professors liked to wear Birkenstocks, and didn't smell very good when you stood next to them.

In fact, studies show that 80 to 90 percent of early on-the-job difficulties stem from carryover college habits, such as dozing off during morning meetings, slipping late assignments under the door, and counting on that one really anal coworker to handle your group work.

As opposed to the self-scheduled days of three-hour breaks between lectures (supposedly to study, but really to nap) and throwaway electives, now your opinions and ideas are the throwaways, with lunch at the desk. Yep, hearken back all you like to when it was hand-slaps and hugs on the way to the library, and a say-so in

Cup-'O-College

Instant Social Network
(just add beer)

how you tackled projects. Today it's averted eyes in the hallways, and prescriptive—usually expired—company methodologies. All presided over by some clown manager who's far less brainy than he supposes, and who doles out work of about the same caliber.

if college students wrote the Bible...

Ten Commandments cut into six, double-spaced, 14 pt. font.

∞

Last Supper eaten next morning. Cold.

∞

Paul's letter to the Romans emailed: abuse@romans.gov

∞

New Edition Bible every year to keep used sales down.

∞

World now created in one day: six resting, one crazy all-nighter.

Otherwise you're invisible to upper-administration, meaning it goes without acknowledgment that you abuse their email system and steal their pens and Post-Its. Thank God, at least, for the cube-mate who insists on those loud personal phone conversations, and the complete inability to differentiate between "polite" and "interested."

In short, you've been Punk'd, with no Ashton to run out and let you in on it. But that's fine; college would've botched the job of teaching you how things really work, anyway—like the parent who sits you down with the illustrated birds-and-bees book. No, this is much more an older brother who hands you the *Playboy* kind of thing.

Still, after seventeen force-fed years, don't you feel a little hypocritical that you're finding your answers today by *reading?* Your communist anthropology professor would be so proud.

Lie no. 3
You're Too Young for an Identity Crisis

Identity is a funny thing. It's basically all we've got while we're making faces at ourselves in the bathroom mirror, yet it teeters so precariously on what we do, where we are, and who we have in our lives at any given point. So now that your access card opens up an office instead of a dorm, it's time to rework the self-concept a little bit. But if we're so adaptable, as Darwin gave the Church heartburn by saying, then it shouldn't be that big of a stretch to go from taking sloppy notes in a lecture hall to taking sloppy notes in a conference room, right?

You bet. About as easy as it is for fifty-year-old men who've quit their jobs, ditched the wife and kids, and are now buying hair transplants and Porsches to get women your age in the backseat.

Dad's Not the Only One Who's Losing It...

"It can throw someone's life into chaotic disarray or paralyze it completely. It may be the single most concentrated period during which individuals relentlessly question their future and how it will follow the events of their past. It covers the interval that encompasses the transition from the academic world to the 'real' world...[and] is usually most intense in twentysomethings."

—From *Quarterlife Crisis*. It's an unnecessarily scientific account, but I'm pretty sure they were worried about sounding legit, so...

Where does that leave you, then, when the second sentence in the conversation has gone from "So, what's your major?" to "So, what do you do?" (Hell, even "art history" goes down easier than "management trainee.") Stripped of your books, your campus, your classmates, and your come-as-you-please attendance policy, you're bound to take a header right into that ugly industrial carpet lining the rat maze you run Monday through Friday. My guess is that some underpaid school administrator, way back when, got slipped a fat envelope under the table from Corporate America, and agreed to play up the glimmer of what lay ahead after college as a distraction from what lay below.

Not like that's stopping you from asking old professors you hardly know for recommendations on your grad school apps. Face it, you're codependent on the academic system—the "battered student" syndrome—and a master's degree feels like a warm security blanket when compared to your scary, yet stylishly practical desk. (The line to get back in, according to *BusinessWeek,* is longer than ever.) Never mind that the fix is just a two-to-four-year Band-Aid, and then it's here-we-go-again into the working life—except now five or six figures deeper into debt, and still looking on Monster.com for something you're now too overeducated to do. And, never mind, enjoy.

It's no wonder why Gen Y is all hopped-up on anti-depressants and moving back home with Mom—and maybe Dad, if he's not out cruising for chicks. But you're *supposed* to be lost and angry and in denial right now; it's the hallmark of your twenties, especially if you're single. The point, rather, is to accept this transition for what it is—the rest of your big, uncertain life—and to hold your friends' hair back while you all puke your nerves out.

> " The teaching profession is the only profession that has no definition for malpractice. "
>
> —Merimon Cuninggim, who I think tried to file suit once

Along the way, though, you'll quietly develop a deeper, more sophisticated sense of happiness and fulfillment as you start to get your legs under you as an employed adult—and, gulp, parent eventually. But yesterday is dead, baby: gone, in the ground, just a Beatles song. So bring a flower, wipe a tear, and for God's sake, stop crashing frat parties. You look ridiculous.

Lie no. 4
Work Is Going to Challenge You Like Your Classes Did

I ronic turn of events, isn't it? Whereas the game in college was to find the easiest classes possible, now you're jonesing for a good fight, a throwback head-scratcher, a reason to call up your coworker at 2 a.m. and ask if he's got any idea what the hell this one paragraph means.

As we'll get into next chapter, Corporate America hires smart people for stupid jobs at the entry level, which is itself both smart and stupid. While intelligent employees have a long reputation for figuring out new and inventive ways to make more money for people who don't really need any more of it, the upkeep is really a bitch: They're usually super touchy and demanding and egomaniacal and get all pouty when things don't go their way—everything you'd end a relationship over in any other venue. And in your case, without a long reputation for anything other than showing up late and not combing your hair before early classes, it's mental drool all over the desk as a corporate grunt.

Again, we'll discuss exactly why a little bit later. But for now, understand that this move by companies to toss their greenbeans the gruntwork isn't just insulting, but actually contributes to that whole quarterlife-crisis bit: School, after all, was hard. Even for people who were good at it. I mean, not counting the guys you waited for in the parking lot—who could out-drink and under-study everyone, and still walk out with a 92 on the final (e.g., my old

In college, there's sort of an excitement/exhaustion balance to things. Sure, the all-nighters suck; but then the paper's done, you drink until they look hotter (actually, no, you just care less), and you stay up all night again, but this time for a better grade. Finally, you sleep in, miss class, and start again. Who says university life isn't in harmony?

roommate, who now, incidentally, does my taxes)—it took intellect and deception to get things done, and that was the point. Most of the stuff you crammed in one end, of course, fell out the other. But all the new synapses you formed along the way by struggling to put two and two together was what kept life purposeful, what gave you something to procrastinate and feel guilty about.

Now match this up against the entry level, where it all comes to an "exacting" halt—as you wake up at the *exact* same time, sit in the *exact* same cube, put up with the *exact* same people, and grind out the *exact* same reports every period. It's boring to the point of Sunday afternoon TV, and most young professionals just want some "hard" back. And what's most difficult, really, is not descending into complete apathy with it, like when you haven't exercised in a long time and all your muscle

> **Nothing is more important to a man's pride, self-respect, status, and manhood than work. But…pride is built on work and achievement, and the success that accrues from that work.**

—Willard Gaylin, from *The Male Ego* (Curiously, he makes no mention of how a person's name influences self-esteem…)

has gone to fat. Part of you wants to go Tae-Bo it out, and the rest just reaches for the bigger spoon. So the true enemy, it turns out, is no enemy at all.

Unfortunately, there's no better answer here than to tell you that three-quarters of what you'll do during your stint as a grunt is (gasp!) gruntwork. I'll point the fastest way out, of course, but not before you lather up some of that elbow grease Grandpa talks about, and start banging out your work with a little vigor and aplomb.

Indeed, the entry level is the place to sack it up like Martha Stewart, and prove that you've got the discipline to do your stretch like a big girl. With good behavior, you'll be out in eighteen to twenty-four months, tops—and then you can go back to your gardening and pathological narcissism.

Lie no. 5
You Can Expect Similar Performance Feedback

This country's system of higher education, when you think about it, isn't that far removed from our lower one: The projects are about as worthwhile as what you could do with some glitter and elbow macaroni; the teachers offer roughly the same proportion of patience and usable advice; and the reward scheme is just as silly and contrived. But without any cool gold stars to stick on your Trapper Keeper.

And it's really those grades that do us in. We've been weaned, after all, on the praise and ice cream money of gushing parents for bringing home a report card that didn't have to be covered up with a magnet on the fridge. This need for over-the-top validation becomes

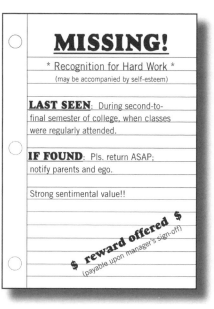

MISSING!

* Recognition for Hard Work *
(may be accompanied by self-esteem)

LAST SEEN: During second-to-final semester of college, when classes were regularly attended.

IF FOUND: Pls. return ASAP; notify parents and ego.

Strong sentimental value!!

$ reward offered $
(payable upon manager's sign-off)

ingrained, second-nature, so that now you're covering up your college exam answers from that guy who you think is sitting a little too close. Besides, the good companies only show their love to the top 10 or 20 percent, so it's screw thy neighbor, capitalism and the American way, blah, blah, blah. All well and good. No, the real problem doesn't start until you actually take rank at the workplace, where the typical atta-boy you get for busting your balls on an assignment is simply the opportunity to keep your job and go for it again next week.

Think about it: In school, after scores were posted and…hell yeah!…you beat that midterm like it owed you money, there was always some partying to be done. Which, if done right, called into question the very basics of your socialization, much less your ability to pass a collegiate exam.

Now at the entry level, on the other hand, the sporadic pat on the back usually means they're about to take credit for your work. And that's poetic justice, really, given all the copyright infringement you got away with during your plagiarized academic career.

Still, it leaves most new grads wondering what happened to Miller Time, and especially during performance reviews—which come but once a year (on the schedule anyway), and which have way more to do with opinion and perception than actual work quality and hours put in. In short, they've done you like Pavlov did his dogs. But now there's nothing to salivate about when the bell rings, and no hot little schnauzer to nuzzle up to afterward.

So since everyone's done patronizing you and kissing your boo-boos, it's time to do what should've been taught from the get-go: taking some freakin' pride in your work! For its own sake, if you follow me—no grade, no lollipop, no football-pat-on-the-ass. We'll also cover this point at length later on in the book, but resolve yourself right here that you're going to go to bed hungry most nights if you don't shrink your appetite for hearty gratitude and credit, and learn to subsist on just the staples of a well-placed thanks and a knowing smile after a hard-fought project.

> " The problem with communication is the illusion that it has occurred. "
>
> —George Bernard Shaw, who, appropriately enough, once lost a job at a telephone company

And even if they're not willing to buy you a beer and make uncomfortable small talk, your tight-lipped superiors still know what's what. So do it well because that's how it should be done, and then shut up about it. Your silence, it turns out, is just what everyone's hoping to hear.

You're Too Smart for This

2

> **From work like ours, there seems to us to have been eliminated every element which constitutes the nobility of labor.**

—Walter Wyckoff, who figured this out, oh, about a hundred years ago...

Lie no. 6
Your College Degree Actually Means Something

Don't get me wrong; you have every reason to be confused. I mean, you're plenty smart and accomplished and potent and all that. But so is every other corporate grunt who just stumbled out of four years of all-night keggers, random hook-ups, and drone-on professors. Many with a better GPA than you. And like anybody will ever ask you for your transcript again.

It's a $100,000 delusion these days for greenbeans sporting a private college degree—that this distinction has, as we just spent a chapter talking about, prepared you to be good at anything other than school. (Which isn't saying all that much, looking at some of the people whose parents get donation requests on the same alumni association letterhead.) Not that most Fortune 500 managers wouldn't rather spend their afternoons over so-so coffee, wordy philosophy texts, and a coed's dreamy eyes. But, like all things wasted on

> 66 **The roots of education are bitter, but the fruit is sweet.** 99
>
> —Aristotle, who clearly never went to college or had an entry level job

the young (and hungover), you can't justify it anymore in the name of higher education or self-realization or any other excuse you used to backpack around Europe for a semester. No, now that you can really appreciate it, you're up late pressing your Donna Karan pantsuits to look completely overdressed while fact-checking and faxing other people's work.

College, it turns out, was just a place to chill for a while, a stopover between adolescence and adulthood, a last hurrah before you knew you needed one. And it's in this context that you should realize your BA is BS—completely meaningless to anyone who has one themselves, and who can write you a check that won't bounce.

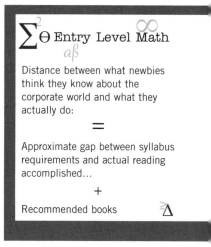

$$\sum{}^{2} \ominus \text{ Entry Level Math} \quad \infty$$
$$a\beta$$

Distance between what newbies think they know about the corporate world and what they actually do:

$$=$$

Approximate gap between syllabus requirements and actual reading accomplished...

$$+$$

Recommended books

$$\Delta$$

Keep this in mind when you're about to casually bring up the fact you set the curve in an upper-division econ class. That only proves you either outsmarted some ponytailed lecturer about Keynesian theories, or were discreet enough not to get caught cheating. If anything, the second one is probably more impressive to your boss. But to think that the resulting corporate offer letter holds water with a grizzled office vet isn't just stupid—it's dangerous.

> **In business, others judge you by what you've done; yet you continue to judge yourself by what you believe you're capable of doing.**
>
> —I forget who said this, but I obviously wrote it down at some point.

Not only because these are the coworkers you're going to turn to most often for help, but because their political clout—the people they've seen, heard, know, and gotten drunk with—puts to serious shame whatever BMOC status you may have toted around back in school: "Ooh, you were in student government…tell me more!" (Visual: chin propped in the palms, elbows on desk, eyes like saucers.)

Remember, what you've only read on Vault.com and helped spread rumors about, company old-hands have actually lived, and usually lived hard. Attempting to equate you and them is embarrassingly naïve, and the big boys will make sure that's well understood if necessary. So leave the diploma back home with Mom and her Windex, and try to show some respect, huh?

It really comes down to who should've known better. In college it was you: Your education, after all, was at best an afterthought to professors' research commitments, and every university needs to keep churning out well-employed grads to keep up their national ranking (pronounced "investment rating") in *U.S.News & World Report.* You were obviously good enough—or alumni-recommended enough—to get into the school, so if you bomb on a midterm, well, it wasn't the prof's job to water down his material. It was you who should've watered down your drink the night before.

At the entry level, on the other hand, it's the company's forecasting f'-up. See, signing on a new grad is a lot like going to the racetrack: You play the odds, giving a better handicap to the kids with internships, and then it's "go, baby, go!" Some do, some don't, which means everybody starts off where they can do the least amount of harm, and then you individually earn your way up

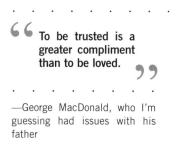

> **To be trusted is a greater compliment than to be loved.**
>
> —George MacDonald, who I'm guessing had issues with his father

from there. So in comes the document-formatting and background-researching and whatever other numbing and humiliating chore they can overpay you to do. (Which, again, isn't saying much. About either of you.)

Formally or informally, depending on where you are, that translates into about ninety days to prove you can keep making coffee that tastes this good. Because if you need too much coddling or guidance with the early stuff, just think what a pain in the ass you're going to be to manage once you dive headlong into major client work.

And it's not only how neatly you can line up bullet points in Word; you're also being judged—much more so, really—on how you look, communicate, get along, and can take a punch. Plus it all comes down to how your manager feels about you anyway, which has far more to do with his professional agenda and fiber intake than your competency or enthusiasm. Kind of makes you misty for the days when you whined about an unfair grading policy. (e.g., "Oh, that's totally a half-point!")

Some Famous First 90 Days:

name: T. S. Eliot
job: Temporary Staff
place: Lloyds Bank

name: Albert Einstein
job: Technical Officer
place: Swiss Patent Office

name: Charles Darwin
job: Gentleman's Companion
place: *HMS Beagle*

Author's note: Not entirely sure what duties a "gentleman's companion" may have carried out aboard ship, but speculate it differs significantly from contemporary interpretation.

Look, your only credibility right now is that you've passed your classes, passed muster with recruiting, and passed the receptionist on the way to successfully finding your desk. People's reputations and jobs are on the line here, so think about how reasonable it is for them to entrust you with the mission-critical stuff straight out of the gate.

The trick, rather, is to resign yourself to the fact that there's not going to be a ton of mystery or intrigue to your day-to-day as a grunt, and that you need to make the prettiest picture for Daddy with the crayons and finger-paints you're given. That's at least until you can prove you're not just some also-ran in this horse (rather, rat) race.

> ### Break It Down
>
> According to the research, you have just seven to ten seconds to make a good first impression. But don't worry; nobody's listening to you anyway.
>
> **50%—Appearance**
> - posture, handshake
> - gestures, facial expressions
> - clothes, hair, makeup
>
> **40%—Sound**
> - tone, articulation, cadence
>
> **10%—What you're actually saying**

Lie no. 8
You'll Be Doing the Job That the Company Described

O f all the items on the bill of goods you're sold by your hiring company, this is probably the easiest one to pick out. Naturally you're going to get pitched the glossy-brochure version of the job. What, you think they're going to level with you, and let all that gullibility and inexperience of yours go to waste? Don't be silly—the Fortune 500 has got enough smoke and mirrors to fool David Blaine, and puts on a far more energetic show.

All it takes is a rented campus auditorium (for free, or at a fire-sale price), some reheated hors d'oeuvres, a flashy multimedia presentation, some over-caffeinated company reps, and ta-da! Watch them use all the right buzzwords to hype (read: lie about) the exciting and challenging work you'll do with diverse colleagues and big clients, and explain (read: make up) how you will receive

" **Men occasionally stumble over the truth, but most of them pick themselves up and hurry off as if nothing had happened.** "

—Winston Churchill, who never accounted for companies being much more careful where they step

world-class training and mentoring from the top people in the firm. They sometimes even offer sweeping promises of travel to exotic destinations, and abounding opportunities for personal growth and professional advancement (read: after you quit).

But, c'mon, look at you: young, educated, enthusiastic, teachable, willing to put in long hours—definite girlfriend/boyfriend material. Plus you're a cheap, low-profile, relatively safe way for the company to knock out the stuff that has to get done, but that it doesn't pay for more senior folks to do. And it's not like the grunt-work is a forever thing, provided you learn fast, keep quiet, and don't leave too soon: Corporate America's "weeder class," if you like. (Although the relationship's been getting shorter and shorter since the early '90s, which has definitely hurt the bottom line, seeing as you're pretty much a break-even deal during your first year or two.)

| $ | $ | $ | $ | $ | $ | $ | $ |

drive off with a shiny new grunt *today*!

Sample Fortune 500 entry-level hiring costs:

Recruiting:	$6,000 - $8,000
Training:	$8,000 - $12,000
"Ramp-up" Time:	$4,000 - $6,000
Total Sticker Price*	**$18,000 - $26,000**

| $ | $ | $ | $ | $ | $ | $ | $ |

*MSRP. Tax, title, and experience not included. Options vary by school.

Still, career freshmen remain a commodity—where the collegiate system is like a giant Wal-Mart. Meaning you're entirely replaceable, if need be, at an everyday low price, guaranteed. Plus it's not like there's any protection behind your "job description," which is little more than a bait-and-switch scheme HR uses to play hell with its young applicants. No, your job is more or less whatever your manager says it is, for as long as he says it is. And seeing how often the stop-drop-and-roll entry level follows any given course, it's probably just as well that your business card is costume jewelry.

So forgive their dog-and-pony show for now, and graciously put up with the "because I had to do it" legacy BS; at least until you can get a feel for the place, and where you may or may not fit within it. You've got loans, don't forget, and will be flipping on your nighttime desk lamp much faster than you think for sexier work. Which chances are you won't want to do, either.

We're *all* too smart for gruntwork. That's not the point. Presidents of small companies lick envelopes. Not to ensure the taste of the residue fits with the corporate strategy, but because they probably can't pony up the cash for an assistant. And if the check falls out, the phones get shut off, and who's the schmuck then?

Not looking down your nose at the menial tasks you're assigned is going to be one of the—if not *the*—biggest challenges to overcome at the entry level. Especially if you turned your tassel with some Phi Beta Kappa, *summa cum laude* distinction (um, like I did), and have been ringing your inflated head off of low-hanging doorframes for the past four or five years.

You've already proven your smarts to some extent through your gainful employment, beating out at least 65 percent of your graduating class, easy. But what you've really shown you're good at to date—

> **Geniuses are wonks. The typical genius pays dues for at least ten years before contributing anything of lasting value.**
>
> —Steven Pinker, who reminds us that even Mozart started at the entry level, and his bosses *really* sucked

memorizing theories, regurgitating professors' ideas back to them in no more than five pages, wrangling copies of last semester's exam for $50—doesn't have any meaningful bearing on the business your company is transacting. Sure, the creativity, persistence, and moral flexibility you demonstrated while negotiating your classes are definitely attractive qualities—that's why they signed you ("buy for potential, train for skill"). But, for now anyway, it's the stuff of understaffed biz owners with overdue long-distance bills.

> 66 **The English instinctively admire any man who has no talent and is modest about it.** 99
>
> —American author James Agate, explaining how your boss got promoted

Again, it's a matter of building up your manager's trust in you—like that next romance after he was cheated on—which can sometimes be up to a yearlong process. Until he's ready to open up then, you've got to bite it and do pretty much whatever he asks, as we've discussed. Pushing too hard too early is a lot like getting into a debate with a professor about a midterm grade: Not only are you unlikely to get what you're shopping for, but he's probably going to re-score the exam himself now, knocking you down another letter grade. Keep in mind, also, that whole Wal-Mart thing—where it's pocket change to flick you into the basket, a hand in the penny jar to train you, and a quick ride back to the store to grab a replacement.

So it's about biding your time right now, sweating it out. You're doing the work that has to get done *today,* so it's your job to prove that you can out-research, out-data-dig, out-spellcheck, and

broadly outdo whomever you're competing against. That's what's going to inspire confidence, and position you for a move upmarket. Faltering in quality, gusto, or patience after just a few months, on the other hand, is only going to quash whatever goodwill you've managed to build up so far. Probably with bruising.

Indeed, put away the condom, my friend—no sex on the first date here. Corporate America, much like your twice-shy boss, is an old-fashioned kind of gal when it comes to putting out.

Lie no. 10
Intelligence Makes Up for Experience

The problem with experience, the saying goes, is that you don't get it until *after* you need it. (Same for driver's licenses and the truth about most ex's.) But you can't outwit it—no matter how smart you are—and if you don't show some deference, you'll get worked over almost every time. (Think Bill Murray in *Groundhog Day*.)

Even with a couple solid internships under your belt and some good entry level exposure so far, your perspective of the working world is still spotty, fractured, and entirely incomplete. The fact is that you can't fully understand it until you've lived it day-in and day-out for a few years. Which is fine, because this is the process; it takes time. But until you can tell

Long on Experience, Never Short on Cash

Former Harvard Business School professor (and personal friend) Dr. Mark Albion tells a story of a gifted engineer who developed a unique talent for fixing machines.

No sooner did he retire than a multimillion-dollar contraption at his ex-company went on the fritz. Being persuaded back in for one last job, our man considered the machine for a day, and left after chalk-marking an "x" on the faulty part. Sure enough, it was humming right after they made the switch.

When the firm balked at his $50,000 bill, however, the engineer sent a two-line invoice. Which was eventually paid in full:

One chalk mark . . .$1.00

Knowing where to put it $49,999.00

when the train's coming before it starts mowing people down, it's essential that you keep quiet and keep your ear to the tracks. You'll see soon enough how stupid you sounded when you first got there.

But it should make you feel better that even multi-billion-dollar CEOs get booted all the time for throwing darts, and then telling reporters and their board of directors that they knew what they were doing. Owning up to what you *don't* know, instead, often earns a lot more respect than faking it—demonstrating an uncommon maturity and humility for someone in your position.

Just so long as it's not about the company's dating policy or expensing your bar tab or whatever.

You Should See a Doctor...

Robert E. Kelley, a professor at Carnegie Mellon University's Graduate School of Industrial Administration, puts his trust in the experience of the ER:

"Think of how doctors work," he suggests. "Over time, they see hundreds and hundreds of patients, they build up a base of case histories, and they learn to identify symptoms that go together."

To be a star at your job, Kelley analogizes, you have to build up your own personal log of experiences, and develop your capacity for pattern recognition.

Plus it also helps to remember that even top med school grads do time as low-paid, lower-regarded residents, and usually can't get a real job practicing medicine before their thirties.

And when you're sitting there all cold and vulnerable in your open-backed gown, you don't want them there any sooner. Screw that hotshot with the top 1 percent MCAT score; I'll take the old guy!

66 **Jazz comes from who you are, where you've been, what you've done. If you don't live it, it won't come out of your horn.** 99

—Jazz great Charlie Parker, nick-named "The Bird" for stealing chickens

Just about every manager ever polled since the beginning of time—or at least since the beginning of polls—has cited "good attitude" as one of the most important attributes a new employee can walk into the workplace with. Right next to "ability to run my errands."

So three cheers for smiles, plus a couple more: First, and as you've doubtlessly gathered, real showings of glee around the office are generally reserved for late Friday afternoons, project closings, free lunches, and managerial illnesses. And even then it's kept to a low rumble. So by spreading a little bit of cheer out of turn, people will begin making all sorts of unfounded positive assumptions about you (once it's decided, of course, that this isn't the aberrant result of newness or medication). Don't make it all sunshine and

> 66 Organizations, like families and people in general, often bury conflicts and seek to remain pleasant and friendly, even though emotions like anger simmer beneath the surface. 99

—Joanne Ciulla, from *The Working Life* (This eventually leads to colon cancer.)

rainbows, obviously—and like you could keep *that* up—but just do your best to be someone that others want to be around. Come layoff time, those sorts of things get taken into consideration, believe me. Laughter, it turns out, can be a life- *and* a job-saver.

Second, when you happily accept your IQ-threatening assignments—albeit through the cacophonous gnashing of your gritted teeth—you're going to satisfy and confuse your boss to no end, suggesting that you might be the one to work his upper-drawer stuff next time around.

Whether that happens or not, though, don't forget that the company is kicking your tires and slamming your doors at the entry level to see how you're built. So if you end up becoming a squeaky wheel, you're not getting oiled; you're getting replaced. Why get their hands all greasy when Wal-Mart's right around the corner?

Entrepreneurs Don't Cry

"Building EarthLink was a fight—a scratching, clawing, tooth-and-nail battle, and I'm glad for it," reflects founder and chairman Sky Dayton. "Being an entrepreneur is hard, and raising capital is supposed to be an arduous rite of passage."

Same for the entry level, but without the pop-ups. Unless you count your boss sneaking up on you.

Lie no. 12
Do Whatever Is Asked of You

This is a tricky one. Probably 9.9 out of the 10 things you get asked to do as a grunt are on the up-and-up, provided it's in moderation. Even on the weekends or at Staples. Ah, but that one time in one hundred where you're going in circles and kissing uncalled-for ass to get there.

There's only an extent to which you should pay your dues, and it's only so far that you ought to bag your pride. That line in the sand is broken and uneven, however, meaning any pushback you throw around has got to be an exceedingly careful judgment call, as with girlfriends and parents.

Start by trying to figure out if there's some sort of method to your boss's madness—if he's got your future on his mind, if he's going to be a champion for you—or if the guy is just killing time between therapy visits and weekend-long coke benders. When you're on a clear

> ### Bullish on Bosses!
>
> "By my second day on the job, I saw the unbridled influence my manager had over my career, and therefore my life," remembers Merrill Lynch's ex-chairman and CEO David Komansky about his first entry level guardsman. "I saw immediately that I was on the wrong side of this equation."
>
> I wonder what took him so long…
>
> —From *Lessons from the Top*

track, with a measured approach to your work-flow and exposure to new material, then just give the handful of unreasonable jobs a shrug: It was even more unreasonable, don't forget, when your manager was asked to do it. Which is partly why you're here today; shit travels downhill.

Otherwise, no matter how much fun your boss may be at happy hour, he's just below Osama on your own little personal Axis of Evil. So be vigilant about things, keeping a sharp and early eye out for the red flags raised by bullying, abandonment, excessive ignorance, and the like. Again, this is pretty uncommon, and part of it is usually attributable to a normal "breaking-in" process, where you're both still feeling each other out. Some managers also make

The Fortune 500 Speaks

"She can't accept that while the research she's responsible for is very important, there's nothing fantastic or center stage about it," remarked an 'unnamed' Fortune 500 manager during a recent interview. "She wants everything to be meaningful and creative and fun, when a lot of work is simply mundane. She doesn't want to do the time in the trenches."

(This is how entry level managers get burnt out, and eventually put you on the receiving end of it.)

you work harder than others to earn their respect, so there's always some bending over involved. Just make sure you don't find yourself grabbing your ankles, if you know what I mean.

66 **You might as well fall flat on your face as lean over too far backward.**
99

—American cartoonist James Thurber, illustrating that lying on your back and stomach are only for sleep and sex, neither of which should be happening at the office (At least not everyday.)

" Don't speak unless you can improve upon the silence. **"**

—Spanish proverb (not applicable to Penelope Cruz)

3

Misconceptions about Managers, Coworkers, and Others Who Regularly Piss You Off

6 6 The secret to managing is to keep the guys who hate you away from the guys who are undecided. **9 9**

—Casey Stengel, old-time New York Yankees manager who probably had a much easier time of this than your boss. At least Casey won games.

You can think of managers almost as a third parent: You get the one you're given, misbehavior doesn't go unpunished, back-talking is risky, and they control your allowance. This individual is also responsible for your training agenda, access to key colleagues and clients, advancement opportunities, and how often you come home needing a beer or a quickie.

So, also like a parent, you've got to make them feel like they're in control, like they've got a handle on you—while you secretly sneak out the window after they go to sleep to go make out in someone's car.

It begins with helping this guy (or woman, of course, but for simplicity sake, let's assume) look good. He's trying to impress his bosses, keep in mind, just as much as you're trying to impress him, and probably doing about as effective a job. So since his bad days usually end up becoming yours, it's in your interest to have your supervisor's back: Making sure that whatever you touch with his name on it is

In One Ear...

Studies show that employees usually retain only about a third of what their managers say.

—Still an excessive amount, arguably, but you've got to move up from college.

done with the same concern and attention that you might afford, say, a strange rash in a bad place. In other words, kind of the way he sees you.

Which usually starts with understanding his expectations about things, how he likes to have stuff done. Not that it's going to make any sense except to him, his shrink, and/or the inane client who's writing the check. But it'll at least give you some elbowroom with regard to how closely you're managed, and a chance to see up close what bipolar disorder looks like.

In addition, then, to doing the one thing you've really practiced for years— writing down whatever comes out of someone's mouth (without the periodic zoning out like during class) and figuring out what the hell it means later— you've also got to put your intuition skills to work, as when trying to predict the book-to-lecture ratio on an

> **So much of what we call management consists in making it difficult for people to work.** "

—Peter Drucker, the Yoda of management gurus

exam, or how many days he actually meant when he said, "I'll call you tomorrow."

Start by looking, for example, at the kinds of information your manager usually pays attention to, what he harps on during group meetings, when he tends to request certain reports, and also his general recap preferences (e.g., when he wants the play-by-play vs. just the highlight reel). The idea, in short, is to think for your boss before he has to. Assuming that was going to happen. Which you shouldn't.

Also en route to building his completely unfounded trust in you is not calling him out on his haphazard decision-making (God help you in front of his superiors). Entirely unlike those spirited debates back in college— where even fantastically dumb comments were politely tolerated—your manager's opinion is the only one that counts. Until his bosses change his mind for him, of course.

Obviously you're going to take issue with a lot of what goes on at the office; I'd worry about your judgment if you didn't. But, as alluded to, you've got to keep in mind that your boss's accountability probably stretches some way up the food chain—meaning he's got to adjust for the political sensitivities of highly illogical people who have the ability to fire him. Just like you.

If you absolutely have to pick this particular bone, however, there are ways of going about it, which we'll cover later on. At this point, knowing what you know about your latitude for grievances, be sure that you catch him on his preferred day, at his preferred hour, in his preferred mood, and at his preferred point in the process. Then you can make your case *once,* and let him do what he will from there. Or, more accurately, won't.

> ### We Like Ike!
>
> "Leadership is the art of getting someone else to do something you want done because he wants to do it."
>
> —Dwight D. Eisenhower

Unless it's a real deal-breaker, such as you becoming a problem employee or quitting (provided that's not a welcome resolution), then don't expect a lot of movement on your issue. Besides, you can probably learn to live with it in time, like a loud neighbor or herpes. That way your political capital gets saved up for the really big stuff, such as raises and promotions and being forgiven for oversleeping. Again.

It would stand to reason that the individual responsible for your time would tell you how to spend most of it. But no self-respecting entry level manager has ever stood for reason. At least not on purpose.

And you're probably just one of a dozen underlings who he has the time and energy to forget about. So don't get all sensitive and give yourself diarrhea worrying that your boss doesn't like you. True, he may not; but the chances are much better that he's just too busy to show you how little he, in fact, cares. Besides, unless you've got one of those sissy passive-aggressive types, you'd know straight away whether or not you were in his doghouse.

Which is both a good and bad thing: Good because your manager's not around to know exactly what you're not doing, meaning you can give the truth a nice rubdown—within reason—when he gets around to asking. (It's amazing how busy you can sound when you rattle off a list of two-minute assignments really fast.) Bad from the standpoint that you can be a week into a project only to be told that you're way off track, and now the timeline may be thrown, and we're going to have to re-scope this thing, and why the hell didn't you come see me?

Remember, it's not your manager's job to ask you what you're doing and how you're doing it. I mean, of course it is, by definition (and he's right on top of things, sir, if his bosses ever solicit any "upward feedback"). But in practice, the onus is on you to pull him aside from time to time to sign off on whatever you're apparently occupied with.

So make it a point to periodically circle back (buzzword alert!) with your supervisor, even if you feel like you understand what's going on with your assignments and think you're making good progress. You have to be right

The Millennial Generation: 1981–1999

(a.k.a., Gen Y, Gen Next, Echo Boom, Baby Busters)

INFLUENCES:

Prince William, Chelsea Clinton, Tinky Winky (?), Ricky Martin, Claire Danes, Kurt Kobain, Barney, Britney, Backstreet Boys, Buffy, Cartman, Marilyn Manson, Venus and Serena Williams, *90210*, cyberspace, "outer space"

COMMENTARY:

"Combine their confident, pragmatic nature with a workplace that hasn't yet made way for Millennials, and you're going to have a combustible atmosphere that could blow at any time."

—From *When Generations Collide*

Chances are your manager is reading stuff like this, and maybe even believing it. If he's older than forty, chances are he's crouching behind his office door waiting for you to go "boom."

on both counts, which you're probably not, to a greater or lesser degree. Plus it's important to show at the beginning that you're aware of the feedback loop (second buzzword, same paragraph!), and are comfortable shifting gears (oh, stop it already!) on short notice.

Maybe even formalize it, if he's amenable, into a fifteen or thirty-minute weekly thing—which will give you some good face time, as well as foster the kind of open communication characterizing a relationship Dr. Phil might not get red about. It'll also afford your boss the time to organize his thoughts about your work; or, more likely still, force him to actually have some of those.

Be advised, though, that some newbies go overboard here, and try to make it look like they're single-handedly holding the place together. Not only is that absurd, but also your manager's job with his own superiors (which he's doing about as persuasively). Just keep it to the stuff he needs to know, and only those parts he needs to do something with. Clearly there's no problem asking when he wants more of something.

> 66 **It's virtually impossible to communicate too much. I've never heard a single [boss] anywhere complain that he or she is being kept too informed.** 99

—Jim Broadhead, former chairman and CEO of Florida Power and Light Group, one of the U.S.'s largest publicly-owned utilities (Note: He was talking about employees when he said this; but all you have to do is put the person you want in between the brackets, and violá!)

Lie no. 15
Managers Just Love Surprises

Y ou know those gestures that are really nice in theory, that you think are going to go off so well—like, say, bringing home a puppy or massage oils? Yeah, your manager is the guy who doesn't want to clean up after it (or you), and so I hope you kept the receipt.

At the office, though, they've got a little better argument than being lazy or prudish. First off, whenever you drop a bombshell on your boss, it undermines his credibility and makes him look like he's not in control of his team. And while you and I both know he's barely even in control of his BlackBerry, this is the masquerade party you're attending, as we've already discussed. So when you're sitting in that meeting and some new information suddenly springs to mind, you might just want to pull your boss aside afterward.

Sick at Work!
Is your manager suffering? Keep an eye out for the following:

"Cranial-Rectosis"

Description
State of having one's head lodged inextricably in one's behind

Symptoms
Blurred vision, impaired judgment, forgetfulness, confused speech, sore neck

Cause
Excessive and unchecked exposure to corporate environments and/or Michael Moore documentaries

Otherwise, you're going to put him on the spot, force him to dance around whatever traps you've unwittingly laid down. And we all know from the holiday party that nobody wants to see him dance. (Plus you'll both do one hell of a tango once he gets a hold of you in private.)

Second, when you don't give your boss enough time before a deadline to review your work, you're taking away his most important role as a manager: editing. Doesn't matter if it's changing words, changing graphs, changing pages, changing the oil in his car—just so long as it doesn't really make an overall difference, and that you have to stay up well into the morning to do it. (My personal favorite is when, after five or six versions, he has you switch it back to how you had it to begin with.)

Still, there are several reported instances of good cause on record, like when political considerations call for omitting or emphasizing certain points, or when someone up top has weighed in on, or changed their mind about, a particular aspect of the project. Things like this usually don't get fully explained to people at your level, meaning you have to take it on higher authority that there's some thin veneer of logic behind whatever it is you're skipping spinning class to do.

Which also means that whenever you're hanging on to something that eventually has to cross your boss's desk, better to tell him far sooner than later about what's going on with it—as often as you have to, in as many ways as you have to, until you catch his attention. That way, if he forgets or doesn't appropriately respond, you've at least covered your ass. Not that he won't still find a way to blame you.

Otherwise, it's all about paying attention: seeing what he's good at, what he's not, what motivates him, what scares him. Then you can really start manipulating the relationship, just like back at home.

The Higher You Climb, the More They See Your...

Results of a recent Career-Builder.com survey show that of those people who are dissatisfied with their boss:

- Think they can do a better job: 42%

- Say he doesn't effectively address their concerns: 24%

- Feel he isn't trustworthy: 22%

- Believe they're being punished for something in a past life: 3%

Where companies are really rolling the dice with their fresh recruits doesn't have anything to do with intelligence or charisma or sobriety. Corporate America's not too big on any of that. No, it's actually just their basic ability to play nicely in the sandbox.

Apart from professors, roommates, and the financial aid office, you can piss off pretty much whomever you like in college and get away with it. After all, you don't say boo to anyone but maybe one or two people in your classes each semester, and collaborating during exams is generally frowned upon (or so I found out). Plus since your transcript is the only thing hiring companies typically ask for a copy of, there's no way for them to know that you were the one who elicited audible groans when your hand shot up during group discussions.

Oh, Behave!

Companies responding to a recent survey by the National Association of Colleges and Employers (NACE) said that the ideal entry level job candidate, first and foremost, "knows how to communicate, interact, and work with others effectively."

This was ranked ahead of GPA, creativity, entrepreneurial skills, and even sex appeal.

So this is where they're looking hardest during those tentative First 90 Days we talked about: Managers want to see how quickly and how well you can assimilate into the group and start contributing—if you can figure out when and where not to step. Doesn't matter if you can crunch numbers faster or make slides prettier than the next guy, better than people who've been there for years. If you're rubbing people the wrong way, you're just going to end up rubbing your backside where the company puts its foot. Which even happens to MBAs. From schools you didn't get into.

Managers make most of their staffing decisions for the marquee projects in this way—substituting the average girl who's going to get along with everyone for the whiz kid who's going to hoard her information and eat lunch at her desk everyday. I'm not saying, naturally, that you shouldn't do what you do best; it's just that you've got to be humble about it, making sure you're not coming off as too cocky or resistant to other people's ideas. Once in a while they'll surprise you, and say something you can totally use later.

It's all politics, so just set the tone early that you're likable and easygoing, and then you can get on with being brilliant. Other way around, and you're liable to watch an influential coworker turn sentiment against you. And then how are you supposed to get people to do your work for you?

6 6 **Ninety percent of the art of living consists of getting on with people one cannot stand.** 9 9

—MGM founder Samuel Goldwyn, who knew the other 10 percent was getting actors to sign contracts they didn't read

Lie no. 17
Individual Performance Comes Before Teamwork

Teamwork, basically, is a bunch of people doing whatever a manager tells them to—which managers really, really like to do. And completely unlike college, where your work quality depended only upon how good of a paper you could download off the Web, in business you're sharing a bed—relying on the team to handle their parts of the project accurately and well, to answer the questions you need answering, to go along with group decisions and guidelines, and to not mess around on IM all day. For as long as you all shall work there, 'til layoffs do you part.

Way easier to get out of a bad marriage than a bad coworker, and bosses will jump all over you for letting one of your teammates fall on their face while you turn in your assignments early, trying to look like the hero. You'll really just look like an asshole, and that's where bad reputations and bad basketball teams come from, *Kobe*.

> 66 **It is not enough to succeed. Others must fail.** 99
>
> —American novelist Gore Vidal, who once ran for office and would've obviously made a damn fine politician

If that's your natural inclination, though, it's entirely understandable; college rewarded this kind of behavior. You wanted the under-achievers in your class to help push the curve down. Today, however, it's about being a good supporter, figuring out what you can do to plug the gaps between what your team is and isn't good at doing. And it's this, not so evidently, that will actually earn you your respect and recognition over time. Mommy's little helper gets the A+ now.

Which doesn't mean that you don't still have your individual objectives and goals; performance reviews, don't forget, only affect *your* wallet. Rather, you just prioritize and filter your initiatives and strategies through what's going to work best for the group. As in love and politics, you've got to give to get.

So take a look at what your team is really there to do—what role it plays in the organization's business, besides inflating expense reports and leaving early on Fridays.

> **One man alone can be pretty dumb some-times, but for real bona fide stupidity, there ain't nothing can beat teamwork.**

—Mark Twain, who would've been a hell of a management consultant if they had those back then

What kind of operating discretion, for example, does the group have (i.e., when your manager says, "This is what has to get done and you need to find the best way to do it," or "This is what has to get done and *here's how* you're going to do it"), and what kinds of formal and informal processes have fallen out around that? Who are the key opinion molders; who has your boss's ear; who do you normally pin problems on; who do you really want to bludgeon with a stapler? Taking a sec to step back and recognize the dynamics helps to point toward where, exactly, you might fit best—where you can make the strongest impact, and still use all the company equipment you want for personal stuff.

> " I would've had to have been a complete jerk if I didn't take the attitude, 'Look fellows, I just happen to be here. I was chosen for this, but if we don't operate as a team, I don't see how we are going to get anything done.' "
>
> —Lou Noto, upon being appointed vice chairman of Exxon Mobil Corp back in 1999 (Now I'm paying $3.29 a gallon for 91 octane; thanks a lot, Lou!)

Do note, however, that the group will shape and reshape as different kinds of projects come down the pike; as people write their long-awaited "screw you!" emails and take off for more money; and as certain people wake up one morning and finally nail down what, precisely, their job is. In this way, figuring things out at the workplace isn't an event, but rather an ongoing process. Like dieting and being irritable about it.

R emember when I said it was better to be liked than to be smart? Well, it's better to be smart when you can't be liked. (Which is how video games were invented.)

For whatever reason—be it jealousy or competitiveness or that they didn't get breast-fed long enough—certain coworkers are just going to have a hard-on for you, and there's not a lot you can do about it.

Still, there are ways to keep this number to a minimum, most important of which being that you share your accomplishments with only those who really need to hear about them (i.e., your boss, your parents, and your little flowered and scented diary). By showing off this accolade and that executive pet-project you're working on, it's even going to make the folks who once liked you try to figure out if it's possible to slip a laxative into your morning coffee without you tasting it.

But this isn't to say, either, that you apologize for your success, or go home at nights wringing your

> 66 **Never interrupt your enemy when he is making a mistake.** 99
>
> —Napoleon Bonaparte, whose advice came back to bite him in the ass at Waterloo

hands about how so-and-so's not going to invite you to the kickoff meeting or her slumber party next week; these are just people you collectively earn money with. Nothing more than simple economic necessity here. So when you let yourself get all caught up in that he-said-she-said mess (which is just what they're hoping for), it's only going to drag you to their level, where they'll proceed to beat you with all the experience they've got down there.

The idea, rather, is to spread the loving around a bit, show that you can give credit where credit isn't necessarily due. In other words, when you shoulder a project that turned out well,

if you acknowledge the team in public for all of their help—like when this one let you borrow a paperclip or that one pointed out you had something stuck in your teeth—they're going to get all warm and fuzzy about you, and want to return the favor. Which usually comes back about double whatever you handed out. Plus your manager's going to see exactly what you're up to, and appreciate that you're saving him all of that morale-building work. (And even if he doesn't get it, he'll at least know that you're not causing him any problems, and that the group generally seems to like you, and, well, perhaps he should too.)

> 66 **It is better to be envied than to be pitied.** 99
>
> —Herodotus, who was exiled back in 457 BC, so I don't know who, exactly, he thought was looking up to him

Look, some people are always going to have an issue with you, usually for reasons only they understand. And sometimes they're not always sure themselves. So instead of trying to placate or going tit-for-tat, just handle your business with a smile. That'll usually irk them more than any intentional thing you try to pull, especially if you compliment them on their hair. Try it, really, it's great fun.

Lie no. 19
You Can Handle It Without a Mentor

You ever notice that the people who need the most help usually have the hardest time accepting it? Pretty ridiculous, if you ask me. And not like they would.

But you have to. This is another one of those pride-swallowers if that's your issue, because Corporate America is too big and too confusing a place to try to figure out on your own: Swarms of frustrated and busy people, a litany of procedures and hoops to jump through, the need to do well with your tasks, a permeating desire to get in and out fast—kind of like the DMV, but not quite as friendly and helpful.

Which is why you need to recruit a tour guide, someone to hold your hand and tell you about all the different kinds of animals you'll see today, and to not giggle when you see them peeing on a rock. So maybe it's more like the zoo, I haven't decided.

Anyway, some of the bigger Fortune 500 companies have taken it upon themselves to set up formal mentorship programs,

> " A friend in need is a friend to be avoided. "
>
> —Lord Samuel, who had enough money to say this

which are a mixed bag, at best. Since the participating managers are usually participating involuntarily, newbies often don't figure into their schedules except during downtime at an airport, or after they've thrown a few back and are loose enough to deal with you. Which is why it's smart to find someone on your own, who you're comfortable talking to, and who'll recognize your name when it pops up on their caller ID.

> 66 Be awful nice to 'em goin' up, because you're gonna meet 'em all comin' down. 99
>
> —Jimmy Durante, who I believe was talking specifically about his rhinoplasty surgeon

Comfort level is a big point: A lot of greenbeans are sometimes apprehensive to talk with their mentor about what's really bothering them, fearful that they'll look stupid or naïve—which itself is stupid and naïve, because mentors already know that you are. They were once stupid and naïve, too, which is why they're willing to help you be less of that today. Unless your mentor actually still is stupid and naïve, in which case you'll make a killer team.

But don't pick an advisor just because they're fun or easy to talk to; you can get that from friends or a stripper. No, this is a business relationship, meaning they need to have some hard years in the industry behind them to really know what they're talking about. Which is also why their boss needs them to stay late most nights, meaning you're probably going to need more than one mentor to annoy.

Which you should have regardless, for a couple of reasons. First, no matter how much they like you and want to help, answering your questions is, as I alluded to, a real pain in the ass when they're busy working, or busy trying to get out of working. Also, no one mentor is going to have all the answers you need (or at least not all the good ones), so it's important to have a few opinions on whatever matter you're dealing with.

Based on how they align or don't, you can match that up against your particular situation and see what works best. This is also a good way to prioritize your conversations, as certain advisors will be better in specific areas than others: Some with political issues, some with career issues, some with fashion tips and who totally think you're cute.

Whomever you end up choosing, however, be sure at least one of them has some pull at the company—which you'll need

" **How is it possible to expect that mankind will take advice when they will not so much as take a warning?** "

—Jonathan Swift, whose advice was to sell poor Irish kids as food

so management doesn't mistake you for the rest of the
office furniture when they're redecorating.

Don't get the two confused: While your mentor may feel like a friend and act like a friend and maybe even look like some of your other friends, they're not your friend. You wouldn't call them up to come over and watch a movie, or paint your toenails together, or babysit your dog. And if you would, you need to go make some more friends.

Mentors, instead, are really useful for things like introductions to important people, putting in a word for you when the good projects are being staffed, and, once in a while, taking you to go get some candy and a balloon when you're suicidal.

So when you're not venting (which shouldn't be more than 15 percent of the time if you don't want them to just hand you the number to the employee assistance program and wash their hands), it's a great idea to talk about the kinds of projects you're interested in—and, hey, you wouldn't happen to

> 66 **A doubtful friend is worse than a certain enemy. Let a man be one or the other, and then we know how to meet him.** 99
>
> —Aesop, who must've gotten into fables after a buddy screwed him over

know any managers in that area, would ya?

Chances are they do, or know someone who does, and setting up a quick hello shouldn't be a problem. Plus, if your mentor isn't just doing charity work by dealing with you, but really thinks you've got something to contribute, it's not out of the question that they'd take the next step and do a little campaigning on your behalf. (Although you've got to stop short of explicitly asking, which would be a violation of your relationship—and Hallmark doesn't make a card for that.)

Yes or no, they can at least give you fair warning about what you're up against with different personality types, and what (and what not) to say to get their attention. As occasionally happens, the department you're interested in may be headed up by a communist or schizoid, and

She's Going Down, Cap'n!

"I tend to think mentors are more adjusters. They help to calibrate and adjust the direction you're going in," says Harvard B-School prof Allen Grossman. "That's often very important, because if you're off course by five degrees, a thousand miles later you're in deep trouble."

—From *How They Achieved*

(Author's note: Actually, that would make them more of a "navigator," because I've dealt with plenty of insurance adjusters, and wouldn't call any of them "helpful." At least not after they left.)

the trade-off in short-term sanity for the experience just isn't worth it.

Still, your advisor can always dump out the more general bucket of advice about any kind of project you're working on: Where new grunts seem to trip, the kinds of political problems this particular client is known for, any procedural issues to be aware of, and even technical stuff, like how to make things fly around in PowerPoint. (It's the "Custom Animation" selection under the "Slide Show" tab, by the way; fun for the whole department!)

But you can't get all defensive when they critique you—and the good ones inevitably will—because that's what you're (not) paying them for. Some of the best value mentors can provide, in fact, is slapping you around when you need it; remember, they only want to see that you go on to be successful. An advisor never knows, after all, who *you* might get to know, and the phone may be ringing from the other side someday…

> ❝ **He gives twice that gives soon, i.e., he will soon be called to give again.** ❞
>
> —Benjamin Franklin, who illustrates why your mentor may let you go through to voicemail

A professor's job to her students, who are paying out the nose, is to bestow knowledge. Or at least to show up and talk for an hour. And for the size of the price tag, you'd think kids would be all over that—like eating your money's worth in the dorm cafeteria (before you realized you were getting fat, and had to diet *back down* to the Freshman Fifteen). But, no, college heads aren't like college bellies, and usually go home fairly empty. The only kind of office-hour traffic you really notice, in fact, is just before an exam or paper is due; or just afterward when, hey, you said we didn't need to know that!

This is bad investing—some of the worst you can do, behind only whatever MasterCard and Visa are mugging you for in finance charges every month.

In the business world, by contrast, living and breathing human beings are easily your most important sources of

Choice of a "Y" Generation

"He trained more people who received promotions than any other plant operator," explains David Kendall, former CEO of Pepsi, chatting about one of his first mentors at a warehouse gig. "He used to talk with me until one in the morning. I'd work all day, and at night, sit down with him."

—From *How They Achieved*, and why David Kendall didn't date until his mid-thirties

guidance and information—with the only downside being that, one, you actually have to go talk to them; and two, there's no scheduled time for them to shut up and leave.

Small price for all the juice you can wring out of your conversations, which vary by age: The guys who've been around a while tend to give you a history lesson, with a perspective from when people claimed to have "not gotten the memo"; younger managers, who are still hungry like you, usually have a good sense of where the business is going, and where your department isn't; seniors are typically up on the politics of the place, and can point out who and who not to look directly in the eyes; even peers, if you give them three guesses, will often pull something from the network that you can stick your name on and pass off to your manager with a note like "FYI" or "running with the ball" or "had some downtime" or something obnoxious and proactive like that.

> **Advice: The suggestions you give someone else which you hope will work for your benefit.**
>
> —American satirist Ambrose Bierce, who sums up parenting, managing, politics, and lovemaking

Be aware, however, that some of what you're told, such as with politicians and parents, is going to be incomplete, biased, misleading, or just patently wrong. And while you shouldn't ascribe to spite what can perfectly well be explained by stupidity, it's important that you do a reality check with the stuff that strikes you as suspect.

Except for your colleagues' personal anecdotes, which are frequently too nuts to make up, and way too useful to discount. What a great phenomenon, in this case, that people's favorite thing to talk about is themselves—as there's always some sort of nugget you can apply to your own situation, as well as blackmail them with down the line when you need a favor.

Check the Return Address First

"Trust not the horse, O Trojans. Be it what it may, I fear the Greeks when they offer gifts."

—Virgil, who reminds us that some advice (often the kind given too freely) should be returned to sender, unopened

Particularly the mistakes they've made, which are now far enough in the past that they can laugh about them, but not so unreasonable that you, yourself, wouldn't perhaps forget to double-check the "To" field, and accidentally email the entire western region about who wasn't wearing any panties at the company picnic (true story). Hearing that one, now I type in the address last, and always make sure my laundry's done.

Lie no. 22
Networks Are for More Established Professionals

Q *uid pro quo* is always talked about like it's a bad thing. But when dirty old managers aren't trading hummers for promotions, this whole mutual back-scratching arrangement is actually pretty useful, provided you've got the right partners. Looking around the office, most of the incompetence you see isn't because the company doesn't know any better; it's that there's an uncle who plays golf with someone, and, "Hey, how about hooking up my grossly underqualified nephew with an overcompensated position of outsized importance and authority? Nice shot!"

Way of the world, fair or not. Talent will only get you so far; it's the people who are going to recognize and *pay* for your talent that are going to make you successful. And since you never know who knows whom, it's in your interest to start getting to know everyone you can. Top to bottom.

The Right Hand Washes the Left

"It is one of the most beautiful compensations of this life that no man can sincerely try to help another without helping himself."

—Ralph Waldo Emerson

This is the power of networking (sounds like a telephone commercial), which is one of the most important things you need to get good at as a grunt, besides shaving regularly. Building effective, productive relationships is how you open up professional channels, and position yourself to gain the feedback, opportunities, and contacts you'll need to eventually do what you really want to do for a living. And get invited to parties.

But it's not always that easy—unless you're naturally chatty and open with strangers, like those kids who are just begging to get abducted from the playground. So start at the office simply by saying hi to the people you don't know; you've obviously got something pretty important in common, so use that as your base. Maybe it'll turn into coffee or lunch. Especially if you're paying.

> ❝ You will make more friends in a week by getting yourself interested in other people than you can in a year by trying to get other people interested in you. ❞
>
> —Arnold Bennett, English novelist whose timeline is a bit off, but whose idea is right (Except when you're rich. Then it doesn't even take a week, and you don't have to be interested in anything.)

Next come the conferences and other industry events, which you can find out about by reading your business's trade rag—probably fanned out across the coffee table next to the receptionist—as well as by nudging your boss and seniors about how they stay on top of things. (Very impressive, very expensable.) From there, one contact will run you into the next, which is just what you want in a network: The bigger yours is, the more it's worth (as my bill from Verizon Wireless would suggest). So to minimize the degrees of separation between you and the people who can make things happen, keep slinging those business cards, and keep having those drinks with guys you can't stand until you get the right phone numbers.

Sound a little crass? Of course it does. It's also standard industry practice. Business relationships are utilitarian first, and anything else second. Sure, you may end up finding a mentor; but more than likely you'll just end up finding a putz with an influential relative, like we talked about.

The Bible in Business

Two are better than one, because they have good reward for their labor. For if they fall, the one will lift up his fellow: but woe to him that is alone when he falleth; for he hath not another to help him up.

—Ecclesiastes

But why should they do anything for you? In other words, what can you offer in return? Good question. Nothing, really. But that's okay at first; you're like a third-world country, where trade deficits are forgiven in hopes that you'll have something worth stealing later on.

Still, don't forget where you sit on these people's totem poles today. They're important and busy and don't want to hear from you more than once every couple months. So just keep it to a holiday card and the occasional email; they'll call *you* when there's really something to talk about. Like that hummer.

The Daily Grunt

4

> ❝ The brain is a wonderful organ; it starts working the moment you get up in the morning, and does not stop until you get into the office. ❞

—Robert Frost, American poet who dropped out of both Dartmouth and Harvard, and was then invited back to teach

Lie no. 23
You Can Still Turn in a "B" Assignment

Here's the thing about details: it often doesn't get noticed when you pay attention to them, but it almost always does when you don't.

And the company remembers—for a long, long time (how, I'm not entirely sure, because they don't always write it down). From there, inevitably, it'll get brought up during your performance review, just like a girlfriend does during a big fight with every single thing you've done wrong in the past year. (How the hell *she* does it, I can't say either.)

Especially at the beginning, when the company is still forming their major impressions about you, it's critical that every typo, error, inconsistency, and inaccuracy gets caught and fixed prior to reaching someone you have to lie to about it. And that includes following directions just as they're given, down to how the document should be printed and bound. Because if you can't even do *that* properly, how can you be trusted with the big stuff? Forget about words and

Presidential Slacking

"My father taught me to work; he did not teach me to love it."

—Abraham Lincoln

numbers at this point; let's see if you can get the catering order right.

It's clearly not a question of skill; Koko the sign-language gorilla could probably sub for you, no worries. It's that most grunts get hung-up on the fact that this work is below them, and so they blow it off, like a paper you rushed through the night before back in school.

Difference is that there's no curve here, nobody who you can count on doing a more half-ass job than you. Plus it's not even really about how you compare anymore. Sure, your manager is definitely benchmarking you against your peers, but it's not like you're going to end up looking good if you drop the ball 20 percent of the time to their 40. The number is zero, because that's what the client is paying for. (Who would probably flip out if they found out someone as green as you was touching anything of theirs at all—and justifiably so, because would you really trust you either?)

Which is a great way to think about it: By nailing your assignments, you're making happy the people who help you get paid twice a month. Who, themselves, get paid in part by what you're doing. (And their money, unlike yours, gets spent on weighty things like sending the kids off to private school and, later, drug rehab.) It's not some idiot Marxist PhD asking you to give him three thousand words on whatever that he has no intention of reading; it's someone who's going to make your manager's phone ring if it's not what they expected or were promised.

And even when you give them what they asked for and the boss gets a call for the other reason, that's his win, not yours. So what if you're wiping his ass for him; just wash with soap and hot water and walk him back to his office. He's the one who approves your vacation schedule, after all, and controls how much you really need one.

66 **The main thing is keeping the main thing the main thing.** 99

—German proverb (Good thing their cars are built better than their sayings.)

Lie no. 24
If You're Good, You Shouldn't Make Mistakes

O h, there are going to be screw-ups. I don't care how careful and conscientious you are—even if you left your OCD medication at home, and are counting the number of vowels in your report. You're going to overlook something, probably the most glaring error possible, and someone's going to come back to you and ask how you missed this. All entry level employees suffer through it (along with most government agencies, and that one friend who you needed to get the story right about where you were last night).

What should make you feel better, though, is that everyone else does it, too—top to bottom. Such is the stuff of humans, and of the corporate ones in particular. Now what you shouldn't do, as we'll talk about in a minute, is scramble to cover your mistakes up, or come off like they didn't happen. You're not going to learn anything that way, and nobody is going to believe you besides. Even when they actually should.

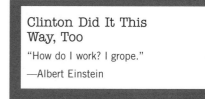

Clinton Did It This Way, Too

"How do I work? I grope."
—Albert Einstein

Rather, you need to look at your gaffes as opportunities to figure out what's wrong with the system—either yours, the company's, or both. Because at that point you can say, "All right, here's where I killed it," and know exactly what to focus on next time. In fact, you need to do that for the stuff you later realize you accidentally got right, as well: Just because the outcome was good doesn't mean the process was. You're only going to pick correctly so many times, as you know from years of multiple-choice exams and bad dates.

Speaking of guessing on tests, there are a couple of other ways to look at your bombs. The first one I'll liken to SAT scores: True, they may be kept on file somewhere, but not because anyone would think—or want—to look at them (except for that "attention to detail" monster, which has a life of its own). In just about every other case, long-term memories in Corporate America aren't very, meaning you're only as good or bad as your most recent project. So it's forgive-and-forget just as soon as you can make them some more money.

The other way to consider a faux pas is by thinking about how long you, yourself, are going to

> **By doing just a little bit everyday, I can gradually let the task overwhelm me.**
>
> —Ashleigh Brilliant, who's right unless you're really busy, in which case you should just get it over with all at once

remember what happened at this place. As we'll discuss at length later on in the book, you'll be up-and-outie in no time, probably within a couple of years, max. So what's the issue with misstepping on their dime?

Don't get me wrong; I'm not saying it's kosher to go hit-or-miss with your job, and your company obviously isn't either. What I am saying is that the consequences of your errors aren't going to follow you around for very long—so, go ahead, test the waters when you need to. Everyone's expecting a certain

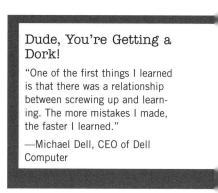

Dude, You're Getting a Dork!

"One of the first things I learned is that there was a relationship between screwing up and learning. The more mistakes I made, the faster I learned."

—Michael Dell, CEO of Dell Computer

number of goofs on your part (there's a budget for it), so why not make them when you're not the one who's really on the hook?

Plus you need to get all the easy mistakes out of the way before you become a manager—a position that has a whole different set of problems attached to it, some clinical. You're going to spend half your time cleaning up all the crap your direct reports turn in to you anyway, so this is also how to know firsthand what to watch out for.

Remember, even the most talented, accomplished professionals, in any trade, still fall on their face from time to time. At least *you* don't have to read about it the next day in the paper.

66 Stupidity got us into this mess, why can't it get us out? **99**

—Will Rogers, who tried to do just that with rope tricks and bad cowboy movies

Lie no. 25
Try to Downplay Your Screw-Ups

Right, so we're all square on how to think about your mistakes, at least at the office. (I don't know how to stop bad dates.) So, what to actually do about them?

Well, as I suggested, it goes against your knee-jerk reaction of pointing the finger, or looking the other way, or quickly fixing whatever you can and slipping your coworker a twenty to keep quiet about it. First off, she won't, and you deserve to lose your money for pulling that. Secondly, trying to blame her or the client or the computer or al Qaeda only wastes time that nobody has (now even less of, thank you very much), and just draws more attention to the problem you want to make go away as quickly and quietly as possible.

> 66 **When in doubt, tell the truth. You will gratify some of the people, and astound the rest.** 99
>
> —Mark Twain, who gives you another way to confuse the hell out of your boss

Now third, and most importantly, everything comes out in the wash eventually, and your little hide-it-over-there scheme—depending on how corrupt and

Errors, Boo-Boos, Yadda, Yadda, Yadda...

John Peterman, founder of the celebrated J. Peterman Catalog (and inspiration for that guy who played Elaine's boss on *Seinfeld*), actually got funding for his company by admitting his past failures. Investors know that someone who's never had to recover from a setback probably doesn't have what it takes to run a successful company—or put up with Elaine's antics.

As Peterman says, "If what you're doing is worth anything, then failing now and then is inevitable."

Author's note: He proved it again in 1999, when his company filed for bankruptcy. But it's still around today and Seinfeld *is in syndication, so there you go.*

impressive—can get you canned even faster than it took you to come up with the plot. Including the time it takes to sign the human resources paperwork and get the rumors started and have the rent-a-cop come escort you from the building and all that.

If we learned anything from Enron and Martha and Milli Vanilli, it's that the cover-up is usually worse than the crime itself. So just *own it*. That's your bad boy, and by being accountable for what you've done, you're actually going to earn yourself a little respect and credibility when everything's over with. Not too many people, after all, have the knicky-knacks to stand up and admit when they were wrong. Especially grunts and managers, who much prefer to…blame it on the rain. (Sorry.)

Still, you don't want to put it over the PA system either, so it's fine to keep the problem quiet until you've really figured out what's going on. Perhaps you can resolve the issue directly with the client—just sending over a corrected version or whatever—in which case your boss doesn't necessarily need to be brought into the loop. Regardless, you have to be able to speak intelligently to all of the questions you're going to get asked, so make sure you've got the facts straight before you alert the media. (Unless, of course, they alert you first, in which case I hope you do better than OJ did.)

Best case scenario, you can turn the situation on its head by, one, using your quick and effective cleanup as an opportunity to impress your boss; and two, seeing this as a chance to plug the holes in your company's approach. That is, if you can show your manager how and where the process broke down (assuming it did), and then recommend a couple of potential ways to do it better, you've just given him something he can look clever about at a status meeting with his bosses. And what a nice change for him.

> **If you think the problem is bad now, just wait until we've solved it.**
>
> —Kasspe, who really understood the essence of management consulting

Otherwise, just make sure that you don't get implicated in anyone else's drama where you didn't have a hand. Or at least get your twenty back first.

Lie no. 26
People Remember What They Said, Asked, or Promised

Forgetting is convenient, and works every time. There's a lot less to do, somehow, when you don't remember how much there is to do. Except when it matters to you, where you won't forget, but they might. Which, in sum, is why your boss is always late with your performance review.

Likewise, he definitely won't recall those just-occurred-to-me assignments he drops in a stream of consciousness as he passes your desk. Until he does. Which are in addition to the three meetings he asked you to sit in on—through a combo of instructionless email forwards and peripheral vision—all happening today at four. On different floors. Only one is actually important, of course. Except when the other two are.

And you're responsible for all of it. Not doing all of it, obviously, but for getting the prioritized list from your manager. Which isn't just what and when, but also *how:* Until you really learn to read him (and even then),

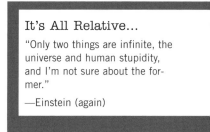

It's All Relative...

"Only two things are infinite, the universe and human stupidity, and I'm not sure about the former."

—Einstein (again)

your interpretation may be wildly skewed from the barely formed silhouette in his head—probably not even close to one of those Apple iPod ads.

Never mind that he may need to see your painfully misguided stab at it to really know what he doesn't want; make him say it first, give you carte blanche with the assignment—in writing, notarized where possible. Again and again, every three thousand miles, until you almost become a pain in the ass with it. (This is a balance you need to strike, and it's different for every relationship. Think of it, I suppose, as calling someone you're just starting to date: They'll let you know, one way or the other, how much is too much. Or the cops will, it depends.)

> 66 **Nothing interferes with my concentration. You could put an orgy in my office, and I wouldn't look up. Well, maybe once.** 99
>
> —Isaac Asimov, best known for authoring *I, Robot,* but who also wrote four hundred other books, so he wasn't completely kidding here

You don't want to guess, because if you guess, it's going to be wrong. Even if you're right. And you absolutely don't want to make an "executive decision," because even executives don't usually do that very well. Just confirm exactly what he wants from you, and then give it to him exactly how he wants it. Happily, the process gets shorter in time as a comfort level develops between you two—a kind of shorthand, where you'll know just what he's thinking.

Now that should scare you a little bit. But it should also make this game of charades a lot easier to play, where you have a pretty good sense of what to get on right away, and how to get on it. Or at least how to convincingly make it seem that way.

Bottom line, it's all about being *accountable:* picking up every last crumb of daily minutia about timelines, project specs, meetings, whatever. Including anticipating what will need follow-up down the line. Which, yes, means calling when you don't want to call, and reminding when you don't want to remind, and planning ahead when you haven't even planned dinner. Because when you fail to do any of these, I promise you that's the one thing your boss will decide to ask you about that day. Which he'll then promptly forget.

CYA File

Acronym

"Cover Your Ass"

Purpose

Kept for when fingers are being pointed at you, and you really didn't screw it up this time.

Exception

If your manager dropped the ball...cover his ass so he doesn't fire yours.

Contents

- When you handed it off
- What they need to do
- Who needs to approve
- When you followed up
- When you called again
- How you were never copied
- Who never talked to you
- Who touched you where

Your manager and clients should know as little as possible, and most of them are well on their way. Especially when it comes to you doing actual work for these people (which should also, of course, be kept to a minimum). Because expectations about how fast they're going to get something from you are set even faster—usually after just one time around. It's like reasoning with a five-year-old about how you'll do Disneyland next summer instead. The place may not even be there by then.

Take Zig Ziglar (real name, cruel parents), who's probably the greatest salesman ever. Not that that's a distinction you'd normally go around talking about, but Ziglar was a genius at keeping his customers happy. Mostly by keeping them in the dark.

See, Zig never showed his hand entirely, always making sure he had plenty of opportunity for upside: a little more, a little better, a

> 66 **I love deadlines. I love the wooshing sound they make as they fly by.** 99
>
> —Douglas Adams, who must've had some really big ones, because mine never make noise (although bosses have…)

little faster than whatever his clients were expecting. And, just as expected, they kept coming back to Ziggy—even if his stuff wasn't appreciably different than what his competitors were hawking. (Plus he totally owned the Z tab in everybody's Rolodex.)

Fine, good for him, what if you're not in sales? Ah, but you are. We all are. As we'll get into next chapter, you're just as much a part of the product as any idiotic crap you're planning to hand in. What's worse than crap is late crap. At least get me my crap on time, you know?

As it pertains to your day-to-day, then, this means tacking a few extra on to your deadlines, where possible: giving you some breathing room, a chance to throw in bonus material, and still enough lead time to hand it in early. I've even asked for additional days when I was already done

Under-Promise, Over-Deliver

It's all about *expectation management*, and it even works overseas: "One of the smartest scheduling rules you can apply is to set due dates that are not just meetable, but bearable," or so it says on the UK edition of Monster.com. "By breaking a big task into manageable steps, setting a timetable for doing each step, and chipping away at the project, you can accomplish almost anything—and with a lot less stress than by trying to do it all at once." Except, I'd caution, for breakups. Do those more like a Band-Aid.

> ❝ I like work: it fascinates me. I can sit and look at it for hours. ❞

—Jerome K. Jerome, English novelist who was supporting himself by the age of fourteen (how, reading this, I don't know.)

with the assignment—knowing I'd get left alone during the interim, and look like a rock star for coming through on the original timeline.

Plus, don't forget, you may need a good portion of those add-on hours for proofing, revisions, and everyday time-sinks—such as people dropping by the cube, unexpected client calls, three-hour lunches, all that.

. . . .

“ Tomorrow is often the busiest day of the week. ”

. . . .

—Spanish proverb, particularly true when you need something by then

So scope bigger than you think, and ask for more than you can use. Because early is now on time; on time is now late; and late is no sale. At least not when they're talking about raises. Or Disneyland.

Hey, this is the approach they teach at Kaplan in GMAT prep courses, right? Plus if you at least wrote something down in the blue book during midterms back in school—names, dates, loosely organized facts and theories, something you remember the professor saying once—you at least had a shot at some partial credit.

And that's roughly what you'll get today for a blank look. In business, people have no qualms about making irrational, almost comic, demands, and fully expecting you to give them a serious answer. It's not like they're worried about hurting your feelings or preserving the sanctity of the relationship—particularly if you don't come up with exactly what you said you were going to come up with. And good luck with that if you came up with it right there on the spot.

Which is why account managers are always so careful about what gets communicated to their customers, for good or for bad: Either they're stopping way short of saying what the company

> ### Except When You Said You Would Call...
> "I have often regretted my speech, never my silence."
> —Xenocrates

will offer (i.e., under-promise, over-deliver), or agreeing to impossible requests that the firm doesn't have a prayer of delivering on (i.e., 90 percent of the time). Which is only your problem when you have to try to make happen whatever they sold. Unless, of course, you were the one who inadvertently sold it.

> 66 **It's all very well in practice, but it will never work in theory.** 99
>
> —French management saying, not unlike their foreign relations policy or stance on women's underarm hair

As I mentioned before, you're not privy to most of what goes on behind the scenes. Which, again, isn't really your concern—provided you're not speculating with clients about what's happening back there. Even if you know, or think you know, it's not your place to say what your company can and can't do. Hell, you're still working on what you, yourself, can and can't do (more on that).

No, in cases like this, just stay quiet and look dumb. I'm sure you've got enough practice from taking neuroscience back in college to pull it off, and this is what you should be doing most of the time anyway. Because there are things you tell some customers and not others, so just leave that to the people who (don't) know what they're talking about. Really, you've got plenty of other problems you can call your own without taking on the guys who have sales numbers to meet. At least they get commissions and company cars and dubious reputations.

Closer to home, the bigger issue is making sure that you're not over-selling your own skills. Which is so tempting when you've got an important senior who's come to you looking for a hand, or catch wind of a cross-departmental opportunity you'd kill to get in on. There's a pretty good chance that it's going to take some specific knowledge and expertise in addition to just legwork. Plus you've got your regular load on top of that, so it has to be a very realistic and honest determination about what you're qualified and have the time to take on.

Your boss has enough sense to only give you what you can handle, because he already knows that he's on the hook for your work—that you're representing him. (At least he's usually stumbled upon the realization.) Seniors and other managers, by contrast, often take your smarts for granted, or are too pressed for time and resources to think that far ahead. Especially when you're nodding and grinning and yeah-sure-no-probleming them up and down.

So if you don't know Microsoft Excel, for example, then don't agree to take on an Excel project. You're never going to learn the program fast enough, and never turn in

> 66 I don't want any yes-men around me. I want everyone to tell me the truth, even if it costs them their jobs. 99

—Samuel Goldwyn, who really knew how to get the most out of his employees

results that are good enough. Much better to say you're too busy, or still "ramping up on that skill set." This level of buzzword proficiency is sure to bring them back later.

As far as ethics go, college is for students what prison is for criminals: You only get better at being bad.

There's sort of an implicit shucking of the morals once you walk onto campus, or at least a really good yoga stretch with them; even if you don't mean to. It's just that that atmosphere is so liberal and permissive when it comes to things like drinking and sex, it kind of carries over into academics and student tax returns. Plus the competition is so intense—knowing that besides being smart, everyone else has their crib sheets, old exams, professionally written papers (and for athletes, it's even on the house)—you feel like you have to take your own liberties just to keep up.

Which in a lot of ways you do, arguably. I don't mean outright cheating, per se, but definitely flavors of it. The attitude is more like gaming the system: outsmarting it by cutting the strategic corner

> " **There is no pillow so soft as a clear conscience.** "
>
> —French proverb, particularly true when staying at hostels while backpacking through Paris

here and there. Plus some of what you see is just so damn creative, you've got to give them credit.

Except now instead of just getting kicked out of school or fired, you can actually have charges filed against you for stuff that didn't seem so bad at the time. Not that you ever saw even one of your classmates get tossed from campus, or will ever see a solitary coworker post bail for fudging an expense report. That's not the point. (And we all still "work from home" once in a while.) The point is that the game, for all intents and purposes, is over. Hey, you had fun and got lucky; that's better than Vegas and most blind dates.

Not to be high-handed about it (God knows I've done my share), but the ethical issue can be easy to confuse. Especially when you're pissed off about all the promises your company hasn't come through on. From that place, there's almost a justification to it, like you're taking what you deserve.

A Venti Problem

The two-to-a-block Starbucks Coffee Company ran into an ethical dilemma back in 1994, when a major frost in Brazil ruined most of the green coffee crop they buy. This was also at a time, if you can believe it, when they were still small and needed the cash.

So what do they do? Buy the cheaper beans—a difference in taste that nobody would really notice—or stick with the good stuff, pay too much, and risk scaring off investors?

As chairman Howard Schultz put it, "We would have saved a ton of money, but we would have had a different kind of crisis on our hands."

—From *Pour Your Heart into It*, Schultz's autobiography (Now if he could only get his baristas to stop BS-ing and make my drink faster!)

But you really don't—whatever they said they'd do for or give you. Those were campaign promises, recruiting BS; there's nothing in writing. Apart from how much you're paid and not discriminating against you, there's not a word in your offer letter about type of work, advancement opportunities, training, none of it. Ethically it's questionable, but there's no legal recourse here. If that were the case, headhunters and managers would have to tell the truth, and I wouldn't have a book to write.

So as you're warming your morals back up from room temperature, keep in mind that the best companies and people in the world got where they are today by being honest with their customers. (As that goes, it's why they have customers at all.) You can still be clever and cunning and walk the

Slave to Conscience

"Fame is a vapor, popularity is an accident, money takes wings, those who cheer you today may curse you tomorrow. The only thing that endures is character."

—Horace Greeley

Truth in Business?

A study by the Ethics Resource Center and Kronos Inc. (who, appropriately enough, makes time-card machines) somehow got employees to admit to:

- Calling in sick when they're well 36%
- Keeping quiet about others' misconduct 35%
- Seeing coworkers lie to customers, vendors, or the public 19%
- Seeing coworkers steal from customers or the company 12%

Multiply these by two or three, and you're actually getting close to the real numbers.

line a little bit, of course; competition doesn't go away. But it's a clean fight now. Leave the cheating to your tax returns, where it belongs.

Lie no. 30
You Still Need a Professor to Teach You

L ike they ever did. Or at least things that stuck with you. In fact, I bet you could count on one hand the pieces of information you remember today from any given lecture you ever sat through in college. Assuming you did that often enough to even need a hand to count on.

Retention, rather, is a decision—as is learning in the first place. To be open to the process, you've first got to determine that it's going to be worth your effort. School obviously didn't make the cut, and that was a good call. But now, for the first time ever perhaps, what you know has something to do with how much you make annually. Not that that's a great reason, on its own, to become an academic after how many years of avoiding it. But it's certainly a better start than needing at least an A- in linguistics.

So the syllabus is yours now, and it's about as rough: For beginners, information is everywhere, and it comes in odds and ends—

> " I find that a great part of the information I have was acquired by looking up something and finding something else on the way. "
>
> —Franklin P. Adams (and also true of new restaurants and lovers)

many of which you won't really have any use for in the here and now. (Which is still better than not having any use for *ever.*) Plus it takes some doing to get at most of the good stuff, including being a little clever and sly about how you do it. There's not a report you photocopy, for instance, that you can't learn something from if you stopped bitching for a second and actually read it. That's in addition to the conversations happening all around you—often about things you shouldn't be hearing—if you only put the phone down and eavesdropped properly, like a good employee.

It's catch-as-catch-can, and this is how you start to make up for all the experience you don't have: stealing everyone else's. Before long, you'll start understanding your work in a more sophisticated way, or at least be able to talk about it during presentations like someone who does. Which is very impressive to your manager—meaning he might drag you along to client meetings at this point, because he

Wrap It Up & Go

Paul O'Neill, former chairman of aluminum giant Alcoa (and big-mouthed treasury secretary for the Bush administration before he got fired), is all for staying on top of new things. "In the best people," he says, "I see a commitment to continual learning. I don't mean education, necessarily, in a formal way, but they are people who are constantly in search of new information, and new ways they can integrate it into a framework that they carry around in their head."

—From *Lessons from the Top* (Good point about being able to take it with you wherever you go; especially if you're a loose cannon like Paul.)

knows you're not going to say anything stupid. Or at least incorrect.

Bottom line, this is your only class now, and you've got the kind of educational freedom that makes for not getting one. So, if it helps, think about your promotion, your next job, your next career. Remember, also, that by investing yourself in the process of investing in yourself, you also stand to meet some great mentors and associates; find out about fields and opportunities you had no idea existed; and maybe even lock in a date for Saturday. People who know lots of interesting info and interesting colleagues, after all, are much more likely to get called back. By everyone.

So take that night class, rifle through that filing cabinet, marvel at some of the crap sitting on your company's intranet. It's time well spent. Especially now that you're not paying fifteen grand a semester to have somebody tell you it is.

> " Seeing much, suffering much, and studying much are the three pillars of learning. "
>
> —Benjamin Disraeli, who's got you pegged except for the studying part

I t used to be that you didn't know what you didn't know, and that was fine. Your beer spilled on a section of the college catalog, you picked a major accordingly (I don't know how you do it anymore now that everything's online), and you stopped learning anything else until you had to take a general ed course, or started dating someone who was studying French Lit.

So now you're out and it's more of the same, except this time your date is in computers or law or something much more practical and uninteresting. And even if you're among the few who've actually gone into the industry you were groomed for—a logical move, but usually about as smart as the choice that started everything—

it's not good enough anymore to be good enough at your job. You've got to be good enough at your *manager's* job. How it's supposed to be done, mind you; not how he does it.

But since that's not happening anytime soon

> **You can observe a lot by watching.**

—Yogi Berra, Hall of Fame player and manager for the New York Yankees, who said stuff like this all the time and made it sound strangely insightful

(for either of you), why jeopardize the focus you barely have on your work? Because management isn't up at night worrying about formatting or research or anything you're not even worrying about during the day when you should be; they're concerned about how they're going to stay in business. Which you might be interested in, as well.

To do what you do successfully, you need to understand it in the context of the people who sleep on eight hundred-thread-count sheets: The kinds of initiatives that are going to be interesting and worthwhile to them; where they're looking to take the business, and how that affects you; who the big competitors are, and what they're doing well right now; whether or not the VP wears a hairpiece, because look at how it moves when he talks.

> " The love of learning and the love of money rarely meet. "
>
> —George Herbert, seventeenth-century English poet. Obviously true if you're a college student; not so true if you just got done being a college student, or happen to be running a college.

It works out, because you're making it your issue long before it really is. And now's the time, because one, it's unexpected; two, it's going to help you predict what your manager needs from you; and three, you'll always be up on who's hiring.

But the company also isn't in the business of teaching you their business; school was supposed to have done that, theoretically. Whatever you happen to learn on their payroll, to them, is gravy, a perk, something else to stick in the brochure. They only care if they can measure your education with a calculator. And your boss is going to be less than blasé about it if your study time is interfering with your grunting time. So, as always, be smart about it, and have a program running you can click over to really fast when someone important walks by.

Unlike school, it's *all* business now (and for your college, it always was). Even nonprofit and sometimes government work. So get your head out of the vacuum and stick it in the boardroom: The better you understand the economics and operations of whatever sensible way you've decided to earn an entry level living, the faster you'll be able to move up—and, eventually, up, up, and away.

Especially at the Beginning

"In every man there is something wherein I may learn of him, and in that I am his pupil."

—Ralph Waldo Emerson

It's not your company to break, after all, so what a great opportunity to learn from watching other people do it. Plus when it gets dull, you can just go back to using the color copier to make fliers for your house party next week. Screw Kinko's, man.

The top people, in any business, always seem to be in the know. No matter what you're talking about. Which can be annoying—especially when you're trying to look hip by bringing up some arcane little piece you found on *Slate*, and it turns out they wrote it. But that's only annoying to you; everyone else wants to sleep with them.

The point is that you were reading to begin with, which nearly all successful people do. And not just the mainstream pubs, like the *New York Times* or *Wall Street Journal* (although I highly recommend both), but a collection of industry rags, newsletters, websites, mags, books, blogs, whatever. This may actually be a bit of wasted advice, looking at what you've got in your hands right now; but perhaps this was a gift or a fluke or something you knocked off the shelf by accident while killing time before a movie. (Which, I might add, is probably more expensive after popcorn than this book.)

So how do the know-it-alls find it all? Some of it, which is also irritating, is

> 66 If you can read and you don't, you're dumb. 99
>
> —Malcolm Forbes, who had magazines to sell

that they're cool, and cool people know about stuff the rest of us don't. That's why they're cool. But the remainder of it comes just from being observant of what other people have on their desks, or what you hear them talking about, or, easiest of all, what they tell you to read and give them a report on.

If the skinny on the industry really isn't interesting to you, then don't spend the time or money (although that obviously speaks to a bigger problem, which we'll talk to death later on). Otherwise, this is the way to stay on top of the latest news, trends, happenings, events, and aggravating industry lingo and buzzwords you can sound like a complete tool using. And, again, it doesn't all have to be business-related, nor should it be; some clever small talk can be just as persuasive when you want to get someone to listen to you. Or buy you a ticket to one of those events.

> **We live in an age that reads too much to be wise.**
>
> —Oscar Wilde (and thank God we're past that point now)

Indeed, this is also a great way to learn about the different kinds of seminars and educational programs going on in the space, which you should be clamoring to get in on. As we'll talk about next chapter, you're just as much a product or service as the products or services your company sells. Grunts are competing in an uber-tight labor market—both within and outside of the company—and the types of skills you bring to a position determine, in large part, whether or not you get it. (The balance, of course, is how much they like you, which they also have classes for.)

Plus milking the organization here can effectively add another $10,000 or more to your salary every year, depending on how deep their training pockets are, so tug away. And some of it, which they'll be happy about, won't cost them an extra dime—such as online tutorials they've already bought licenses for, or conferences they get free passes to through one of their vendor or customer relationships. Personally, I know the most important training I ever took was a silly computer-based program that taught PowerPoint. My manager made me do it (on a Saturday, no less, which nearly got her car keyed), and it's absolutely carried me ever since, lucky for her.

> ### Go for Two Lines, If You Can
>
> "Resolve to edge in a little reading every day, if it is but a single sentence. If you gain fifteen minutes a day, it will make itself felt at the end of the year."
>
> —Horace Mann

It may be a hard sell, though, if it's not directly applicable to your job today. Tomorrow doesn't always come for newbies, and you often can't justify the classes you really want. Which is a funny thing to say, given how you feel about classes.

Branding
Your Grunt

“ **No task is so humble
that it does not offer an
outlet for individuality.** ”

—William Feather, who probably would've
admitted that the corporate entry level
comes pretty damn close

A part from being selective about which schools they send their recruiters to, companies can't really tell the difference between grunts. Most of them, in fact, are convinced there isn't one, and in a lot of ways they're right: By and large, newbies all look alike, sound alike, act alike, piss and moan alike, and can get just about anything wrong if you give them enough time and distance. Kind of like the companies themselves, so you'd think the kids would be more recognizable.

Regardless, once you move far enough forward in the courtship process, the wine and roses kick in because they've now determined you're desirable enough to be talking to other employers. Which, if you're smart, you are, because Corporate America is not the place for monogamy. Where else, after all, can you tell your significant other that you've got someone who's offering you more money and perks, and they've got two days to match it or lose you?

> 66 I always wanted to be somebody, but I should've been more specific. 99
>
> —Comedienne and actress Lily Tomlin, who gets to try again with each movie

So the company will wow you and finesse you and maybe even buy you a steak—talking about how special and unique you are, and how this is a place where you'll be challenged and rewarded, and where the people care deeply about your success and future (if not your arteries or waistline). You get seduced, you sign, and before the ink dries...you're sent a cheap token gift, a prewritten welcome note, a delayed start date, a raft of policies, and a six-digit employee number. Welcome to the firm. Back of the line, please.

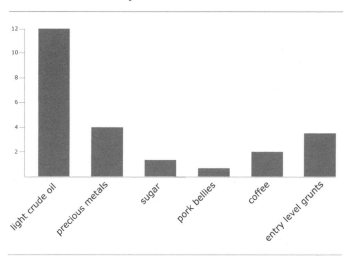

major u.s. commodities

One-of-a-kind? Only to your parents. To the company, you're one of many. Just another warm body, really, in their cloned collection of newbies. Each doing the same kind of gruntwork (in their own vastly important and unique way, of course), and any of whom is easily replaceable when the numbers work out. In fact, if you were being traded on an exchange—which isn't to say you're not—you would be considered a *commodity:* A bulk product that's low priced, indistinguishable from its counterparts, and not highly valued except in large volume. Kind of like college hook-ups.

So where does that leave you, besides stuck at your prefab 5' x 7' cube? (Where, if you put another name in the little placard for fun, I bet most people would start calling you by it.) It's not a good spot unless you can start to stand out, and for the right reasons. Which you can do, actually, in the same way your company did for you: by building a brand. Except you're going to make it happen without an advertising budget, or a PR company to explain what happened, or an industrial paper-shredder for when they can't.

> 66 **Individuality is either the mark of genius or the reverse. Mediocrity finds safety in standardization.** 99
>
> —Fredrick Crane, explaining how your manager keeps his job

I'm saving you a good $80,000 in business school costs with this upcoming branding lesson, so read carefully. You don't want to waste your tuition *again.*

Lie no. 34
Just Blend in with the Crowd

We all know what brands are, at least from a consumer's perspective. The best ones are easy to spot, have a certain quality and style, and show what we're willing to spend to impress people we'll never actually meet.

More specifically, though, a good brand knows what it is and what it isn't. Mostly what it isn't. Because every year, more than twenty-five thousand new products are thrown out there—and about 80 percent of them are "me too"-type deals. Which is also probably why nine out of ten hit the scrapper within two years of hitting the market. Just like grunts do with their first companies.

So if your brand is nothing else, it has to be *different.* And I don't mean different in an "Oh, he must be special" kind of way; I mean different in a, "Wow, I've never seen it done like that before" kind of way. Which you can absolutely do with your cookie-cutter assignments, given a little creativity and sleep deprivation.

> " Regardless of circumstances, each man lives in a world of his own making. "
>
> —Josepha Murray Emms, who's talking especially about writers, and less about shrinks, who live in other people's worlds

Value This

Young & Rubicam, a leading global ad agency, was wondering what makes one brand better than another, and decided to develop this imposing-sounding thing called the Brand Asset Valuator (lovingly called "BAV").

It's a database of more than thirteen thousand brands in thirty-three countries (which takes about as many computer nerds to keep running, I'm guessing). Anyway, they picked the thirty-five most important dimensions of a brand to look at—we take their word there are that many—and ran a bunch of complicated and impressive mathematical formulas.

The one big "ah-ha": Strong brands are strongly differentiated.

I could've saved them *sooo* much money.

And also some marketing—seeing as most people would agree that gruntwork takes a long time and "sucks for you," but would stop short of saying it really counts for anything important. Until, of course, you screw it up, and then see how little it matters. Not that you're going to sell anything like that.

No, even though all you newbies are basically doing the same thing, you're going to be the newbie who does it less basically. And still gets it collated right.

. . . .

66 **Individuality is everywhere to be spaced and respected as the root of everything good.** 99

. . . .

—Jean Paul Richter, who said this too long ago to add, "and the root of bad websites"

value of global brands (1999, so give or take a few billion)

Rank	Brand	Total Brand Value	Value of Brand Name Alone
22	BMW	$11,300,000,000	77%
28	Nike	$8,200,000,000	77%
36	Apple	$4,300,000,000	77%
43	IKEA	$3,500,000,000	75%
N/A	Career Freshman	$147.00	100% (all in the name, baby!)

— From *Brand Leadership*. Measured by Interbrand, except for the last one, obviously.

Lie no. 35
Try to Do Everything Well

If you're lucky, you've figured out the one, maybe two things you can pull off better than most people. And if you're really lucky, you're actually making a living at it. And if you're JLo, you're making more than everyone and not being that good at any of it.

As far as this pertains to you in the office, it means being good at everything you're expected to do, but being amazing at some of it. Which you naturally will be. And the keyword here is *naturally*. I mean, there are certain areas we'd all like to distinguish ourselves in, but it doesn't really work like that. And thankfully, because otherwise there would be way too many actors and musicians and STDs.

And it's not necessarily a whole discipline you need to master, like copywriting or dry-cleaning retrieval; not here, anyway (we'll talk about this later). Rather, just try to focus on certain parts of your personality that really shine through, and that you can hang your hat on (buzzword-a-riffic)! As Dr. David Aaker

> 66 I don't know the key to success, but the key to failure is trying to please everybody. 99
>
> —Bill Cosby, who leaves that to Jell-O and their Pudding Pops!

explains in his book *Brand Leadership,* "The difference between good and brilliant cannot be overstated. The challenge is to be noticed, to be remembered, to change perceptions, to reinforce attitudes, to create deep customer relationships." In short, there are heaps and piles of newbies everywhere—a nameless, faceless mass of young professional humanity—and you've got to be the one grunt that people have a memorable, rewarding experience with. However you can best make that happen. Morally.

It's through this mind-set that you'll really begin to understand what your customers (e.g., boss, clients, colleagues) want and need; where and how your teammates (i.e., competitors) are delivering; and what characteristics you can emphasize and develop to best call out

What's Your Bag, Baby?

Ultimately, you want people to say, "Oh, that's the one who's really good at [blank]." You've got to manage that impression, though, so you don't end up with "leaving early" or "[blank]-ing up directions." So here's a small menu of brand attributes you can potentially pull off:

Results-Oriented

- Resourceful; effective; end purpose in mind; can BS with the best of them

Approachable

- Easy to deal with; relationship-focused; accepts drinks from strangers

Dependable

- Does what it takes; comes through every time; drives a Japanese import

Credible

- Honest; earns confidence; extends boundaries through trust; quitting soon

Influential

- Knows how to approach issues; has sway among peers; "sex as a weapon"

the unique and relevant value set you strategically deliver. And stuff like that.

Don't forget, though, that while it's all well and good to have a high-level vision for yourself, what you're really about is communicated in the mundane: how you handle phone conversations, write emails, carry yourself in meetings, change the toner cartridge in the printer, all that. So start small and work your way up. But literacy and consciousness you've definitely got to nail, first day.

Like That Australian Idiot

"An appeaser is one who feeds a crocodile—hoping it will eat him last."

—Winston Churchill

Lie no. 36
People Already Know What You Can Do for Them

It's astounding how little people actually know. Not that they're stupid in the conventional sense—and not to take away from those who blissfully are, and whom you may or may not report to. It's just that so much of what we assume others know, they really don't. Some of it, to their credit, is bad communication; with other things they perhaps made an active decision to remain a mental no-show. Mostly, though, people are just busy and lazy, meaning you've really got to hit them over the head with your message. And then explain to them that you just hit them over the head.

What we're talking about here is a *brand promise,* or the kinds of functional and emotional benefits your customers can expect to receive when working with you. (Author's aside: I'm not blowing smoke here; this is absolutely the language that marketers use to blow their own smoke.)

> " In proportion to the development of his individuality, each person becomes more valuable to others. "
>
> —John Stuart Mill, nineteenth-century libertarian, and where Ralph Nader probably got most of his ideas

So, to elaborate a bit, a functional benefit deals with the hard, tangible stuff: good quality, on-time delivery, solid follow-through and accountability, and so on. Emotional benefits, on the other hand, go beyond the black-and-white of the work itself, into how the customer feels about it—in this case, *you.* Will your manager, for instance, rest easy and feel validated for trusting you, or will you screw him over like his ex-wife did with the alimony? Are you usually flexible and easy to deal with, or do colleagues get complimentary tickets to a Broadway show with every minor change request? Does being associated with your assignments confer credibility and respect, or does it prompt a spontaneous, "Oh shit, so-and-so worked on this?"

Communicate all of this effectively, and out falls *brand loyalty,* which is the point of everything. You want people to line up for you when the big projects are being staffed, and to provide a vouch when you inevitably drop the ball with something important.

Which will happen a lot more often, do note, if you overextend and try to stretch your brand promise too thin. Once more, good brands know who they are—what they do well, and what they send over to their strategic partners (for a 10 to 15 percent referral fee)—so be careful about what you agree to take on. If you're not going to blow them away, blow them off in the nicest way you can. You've doing both of you a favor, even if only one of you knows it.

The 80/20 Rule

Back in the early 1900s, Italian economist Vilfredo Pareto came up with a mathematical formula to describe the unequal distribution of wealth among people. (We know, obviously, which side of town he lived on.)

Called the Pareto Principle, it was too difficult to pronounce, and so now we just call it the 80/20 Rule. In short, this says that 20 percent of something will end up having 80 percent of the effect.

You can see it everywhere: 20 percent of customers responsible for 80 percent of revenue; 20 percent of employees causing 80 percent of the problems; being good 80 percent of the time and getting caught for the other 20 percent.

As far as your brand is concerned, it means focusing 80 percent of your effort on 20 percent of the people—the ones who are most likely to pay out in the end. This includes your boss, of course; big-time seniors; important managers in other departments; the one or two execs you have access to; the one who actually smiled at you, and not their smoking-hot friend.

Madison Avenue repeats itself a lot, and not just because advertisers like to hear themselves talk. It's that nobody's listening.

See, if they don't bombard you with a message at least seven to nine times, they're not even going to move the needle (buzz that word!) in terms of brand awareness, much less purchase intent. The only way to get busy, lazy, and semi-stupid customers to buy stuff, it turns out, is to do what Mom did to get you to brush your teeth.

And the most useful part of this laziness, as far as your personal brand goes, is how the idea of *familiarity* plays into it. People, after all, just love things they know— accounting for most long-term sufferers of bad jobs, dysfunctional relationships, and Mel Gibson movies. At the office, then, this means getting known and wanted by everyone who matters. Including their assistants, who matter more than you think.

> 66 **Doing business without advertising is like winking at a girl in the dark. You know what you're doing, but nobody else does.** 99
>
> —Stuart H. Britt, who might've tried grabbing her tush and blaming it on someone else

The effect is both direct and indirect. First off, when you're top-of-mind with important and sexy people, that often leads to important and sexy work. Second, when you're just generally regarded around the place, your name is much more likely to get mentioned during discussions with important and sexy people—leading us back to the first point.

And you do it just by saying cheese: In smiling at the people you meet in the kitchen and Xerox room (which is your turf to defend anyway), you're laying the groundwork for a future dialogue, if you don't end up having one right then and there. You never know who they are, remember, or what they can do for you (vice versa, really)— whereas there's always time later to boldly consult your watch, or to finally appreciate

Like a Virgin

Virgin, in addition to being the most provocative, is one of the strongest brands in the world. There's just something about it that makes it memorable and relevant and kind of a turn-on. What are they doing to get us all hot and bothered?

The Virgin Brand Identity

- Service quality; innovation; value
- Fun and entertainment
- The underdog

The Virgin Brand Personality

- Flaunts the rules
- Outrageous sense of humor
- Willing to attack the establishment
- Competent, high standards

The Virgin CEO

- Posed on billboard next to nude models for publicity
- Launched new-wave '80s bands like Culture Club and OMD
- Owns some hundred companies, including airlines, cell phones, and condoms
- My hero

—From *Brand Leadership; Losing My Virginity*

> **If you wish to forget something on the spot, make a note that this thing is to be remembered.**

—Edgar Allan Poe, who is speculated to have died of rabies, and perhaps tried to remember his doctor's appointment

the quasi-inspirational artwork collecting dust on the walls.

Keep in mind, the workplace is a tangle of associations and relationships, and you might just be cold-shouldering the nephew of a big A&R guy over at Sony Music. Now had you only casually struck up a conversation—being friendly, nothing else—you might've found this out, and potentially had an in at a much better way of grunting your way through the entry level. But, no, you had to be all aloof and standoffish, so you deserve to spend your afternoon proofreading. And if this goes against the sensibilities of anyone from a big city like LA or New York…that's my point exactly.

So back to our busy, lazy, and marginally stupid customers: If you try to tell them two things, they'll remember neither of them. One message, you've got a shot, provided you say it again and again; but two, fuggedaboudit. Businesspeople can't even remember half the stuff their managers ask them to do, much less whatever bunk you're trying to peddle. At least with the boss they've got an incentive to pay attention, whereas you're not going to publicly humiliate them if they don't.

Which is why you've got to clearly articulate your *value proposition* in your work, or your unique and important reason for being. This is another darling with the marketing set—targeting the motivations and tastes of your core audience, and explaining exactly how you intend to go about satisfying them. But the focus has to be on just one area, or *niche,* that you know you can do some

> 66 **If one or two people tell you you're an ass, you can ignore them. But if three or four people tell you you're an ass, you may consider putting on a saddle.** 99
>
> —Yiddish saying (except when it comes to literary agents, where you need at least a hundred to really take it seriously)

damage with, and also defend against would-be gatecrashers.

The way to start is by looking around, and then looking at you: First off, you need to determine what your manager and colleagues really need, and who, if anyone, is giving it to them right now. (Like a bad relationship you're eager to break up, so you can move in and treat them right.) Then you've got to decide if this is something you can make a name for yourself with, or even want to. As we'll talk about next chapter, you're only as brilliant as you are profitable, so if it doesn't make dollars, it doesn't make sense. (Corny, I couldn't help it.)

You don't have to reinvent the wheel, though, and probably shouldn't. If people are informally turning to someone in your group right now for, say, market research, they probably aren't doing a bad job with it—and it's not like there are so many ways to do research. Talk to them a little bit, then butter them up for their secrets, see what you can do at a forty-five-degree angle that would make a meaningful difference. Maybe you know someone who has a password for

Same for Winning Auctions

"I've seen a lot of companies fail for lack of focus. I've rarely seen a company fail for being too focused."

—Robert Kagle, founding partner of Benchmark Capital, which funded companies like E-LOAN and eBay and other e-things

Forrester Research or something, and can quietly pull the professional stuff and start to stand out that way. I know you've got enough experience paraphrasing other people's work.

Once you begin to establish yourself as the go-to guy or girl in this area, word will spread— meaning you've got entry points into other departments, as well as relationships with the various movers in the company.

> " When I was younger, I struggled against, you know, 'I don't want to be pigeonholed.' Basically now you want to be pigeonholed. It's your niche. "
>
> —Joan Chen, who struggles against, you know, being a sellout

And now that you have some street cred around town, people will figure that since you're good at this, you're probably good at other, more important projects. Some that even require use of the frontal lobes.

Plus, going back to that whole familiarity idea, your phone is much more likely to ring because they already know and like you. Only thing you need to watch out for, really, is that this doesn't eat into the quality of your other work. Well, that and the elbow of whoever you stole the gig from.

Corporations spend ungodly sums on endorsements. (Nike, for instance, is into NBA star LeBron James for $90,000,000.) The checks are getting so big, in fact, that even Hollywood names are edging into the commercial racket. And who doesn't want to "Get More" when Catherine Zeta-Jones is offering?

That's who you need talking, though, if you want to get the attention of busy, lazy, and vaguely stupid customers. Who are much more apt to give credit when there's a recommendation from someone they recognize, respect, and trust. There are people in your company just like that, and you need them to do that for you. For free, no less.

Well, almost. What you've got to demonstrate is that you're someone worth being associated with—who will serve as a resource to this individual when they're

Halo Effect

The crazy human mind works, in large part, by associations. For instance, we commonly believe that attractive people are also smarter than others. You only have to hang out in a bar for an hour to know this is complete bosh, but it's how we're hardwired.

Put this to work at the office ASAP by ingratiating yourself with a superstar. Their "halo" will rub off as you piggyback on their goodwill and credibility. Suddenly their positive attributes are yours, and without all the hard work!

out serving other people. Because that's what "Midases," as I like to call them, do: touch people and projects all over the place and make them golden. Insofar as they can be in a corporate office, anyway.

Which they'll only do for you once you've built out your niche and are starting to perform at a consistent level. Because it's then that they can recommend you to someone and not jeopardize their reputation. Or so they think.

So where can you look to prove them wrong? Easy—just keep an eye out for the people who get called to fix broken projects, who tend to get brought up as a reference, and who normally have other folks shut up and listen when they're talking.

> " In modern times, it is only by the power of association that men of any calling exercise their due influence in the community. "
>
> —American statesman and Nobel Prize winner Elihu Root, whose "modern times" were the early 1900s

More often than not, these Midases are also pretty easy to deal with, meaning if you approach them with something—including asking for a mentorship—you're probably going to get helped, even if they have to hand you off to someone else.

And don't feel bad. This is great from a networking perspective, and also in terms of gaining that endorsement, which is the next step beyond a passive association (e.g., just being seen talking to them, or dropping their name in a conversation, or getting noticed in the bushes outside of their apartment).

If these are the people management is consulting about important staffing and promotion decisions, and your name is mentioned, that right there can be a major career turning point. And then before you know it, you'll be pitching hair care products when you can't find any good scripts.

> ❝ When you meet some-one better than your-self, turn your thoughts to becoming his equal. ❞
>
> —Confucius, who I'm guessing never had this problem

Lie no. 40
Brands Take Care of Themselves

Nothing takes care of itself, as we've all learned from house pets, dead plants, and failed relationships. Things need feeding and watering and communication, again and again, if you want them to hang around. Same holds for your personal brand, but more so—because at the office, someone else has likely got their eye on your stuff, and doesn't mind walking it at 6 a.m. if they have to.

And even if nobody's out there right now doing it better than you, what's to say that the organization will continue to support your efforts? Corporate priorities come and go like newbies do, and if you're not constantly reevaluating and reinventing your brand, you'll get beaten or become stagnant (and then, possibly, get promoted to senior management). So, like all good brand managers do, you've got to ask yourself every season, "What is it that makes my stuff distinctive, exciting, and relevant?" (Which, for them, is usually followed by, "Still nothing, huh? All

> 66 **If you want to truly understand something, try to change it.** 99
>
> —Kurt Lewin, who didn't want to pay $32.95 at Jiffy Lube again

right, get Catherine Zeta-Jones's agent on the phone again.")

Without the cash to blow on mindless thirty-second TV spots, you instead have to tap your network to keep abreast of how the business is shifting, and where you might go in response—particularly as you mature into more sophisticated areas. By repositioning yourself to focus on this new kind of work, moreover, not only do you ensure you stay valuable to the organization, but that you continue to stay ahead of your rivals. Even the ones who get up earlier than you do.

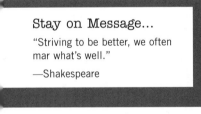

Stay on Message...

"Striving to be better, we often mar what's well."

—Shakespeare

There are two points to keep in mind, however. First, don't lose yourself in trying to be better. The company's interests may have shifted, yes; but that doesn't mean you're necessarily going to be able to satisfy them. Keep doing what you do well, and make an honest, reasonable determination about where you can stretch and where you can't. (If you've ever tried yoga, and then walked gimpy for a week, this idea should be clear to you.)

Second, and more commonly, you've also got to keep an eye on your brand associations: You're on the outside of the good circles at this point, meaning your closest link is to the copy room, bad coffee, and fellow grunts giving lip. Only so much you can do about that right now. Still, you want to distance yourself from the newbies who you know are having their emails read by HR.

> 66 **Another flaw in the human character is that everybody wants to build and nobody wants to do maintenance.** 99
>
> —Kurt Vonnegut, American satirist who's made a living off of flaws in the human character

Which isn't to say you don't have a laugh together, and especially at their expense; just know when and how to keep it in check, like your drinking and farting. Ha, and you thought school didn't teach you anything.

Lies, Damn Lies, and Office Politics

66 Dear, never forget one little point: It's my business. You just work here. 99

—Cosmetics heiress Elizabeth Arden, talking to her husband

The company does what it says it does just like boyfriends do: Ask him what he did last night, he'll say nothing. Ask the company who they're planning to layoff, they'll say nobody. Both of them are full of shit, and you should know better.

You'd do well, in fact, to actually think of the organization as someone you're dating. It's got its own personality, habits, likes and dislikes, skeletons in the closet, executives in the closet. And, just as they're uneasy about you playing nicely with your coworkers, the company is also worried that you won't pick up on all of its quirks and foibles and little looks it gives you. They can't very well stick it in the orientation binder: "Um, yeah, technically that's what the org chart says; but he's just a figurehead, couldn't find his ass if he sat on it. No, no—if you want to get anything done in that department, go see so-and-so. He's the one who's running things down there."

> 66 Politicians are the same all over. They promise to build a bridge where there is no river. 99
>
> —Former Soviet Communist Party leader Nikita Khrushchev, who, for once, made sense

This is the way companies *really* work: "Right" doesn't mean "correct," power has nothing to do with intelligence, and corporate communications managers get their inspiration from the "New in Fiction" table at Barnes & Noble. So you've got to figure out what's what around this place on your own: Who's making nice to whom, and what they're angling for; how things get moved through the system not on paper, but *in practice;* which managers are calling the shots, and which are calling their headhunters. These are the kinds of questions that'll help you understand whom to ask out to lunch, whom to ask for assistance, and whom to ask for their Herman Miller desk chair once they get fired.

Indeed, movement within the company (and sometimes out of it) is directly reliant upon how well you can play the game. And as we'll cover in a minute, you shouldn't be playing at all. I'm just talking about the requisite stuff here—the kinds of issues you can't avoid, like sensitivities with certain people and projects,

You Sure about That?

Robert E. Kelley, our favorite Carnegie Mellon professor who's up on which physician to call when he's got "issues," also knows one or two things about corporate politicking.

"It means understanding the lay of the land in an organization," he explains. "Part of it is knowing whom to trust and whom to avoid. Part of it is knowing how to navigate all of the competing interests within the organization—recognizing which ones will come into play, and which ones you can safely ignore."

All I'd add is that, just like these "issues," don't make a habit of ignoring things. Better to catch it before it spreads. Especially to someone else.

and PR mistakes you need to smooth over. Every project, for example, has certain political hot buttons and egos to manage, so it doesn't matter how you're used to doing things, or what's on the company books. What matters is what's at stake, who's on the hook, who's watching, and how things ought to be done according to whom. Except you.

So just ask: your manager, seniors, peers, Midases, however many ears you need to tug on. You'll probably get just as many answers as people you approach, and that's fine; prioritize by pecking order, and account for the differences as you deal with everyone.

> 66 **In America you can go on the air and kid the politicians, and the politicians can go on the air and kid the people.** 99
>
> —Groucho Marx, who was a lot smarter than people give him credit for

Confusing, yes. Still, not much harder than dating a few people at once: A lot to remember, but doable if they're not friends.

*J*erry Maguire sums this one up pretty well: Put your little moral epiphany into your boss's inbox, and suddenly you're taking the goldfish on your way out. Although if Renée Zellweger comes with, maybe it's worth it, I don't know. Anyway, it speaks to the importance of not speaking—at least not when you're pissed off, or haven't thought things completely through, or if it happens to be a day when the sun comes up.

Your thoughts and opinions, as if they matter to anyone but you and Grandma, are disposable enough when you're actually making a valid point. But to give them a tangible, rereadable, distributable constitution when you're all foamed up? Now that's a special kind of stupid.

The upside of the written word, though, is that it gives you the chance to be reflective about what you've said, if you only slow down for a sec. The self-destruct button (i.e., "Send") is just a

> **If you are patient in a moment of anger, you will escape a hundred days of sorrow.**
>
> —Chinese proverb, developed after enough sore backs from sleeping on the couch

mouse-click away nowadays, so please: give it the hour, the day, the week—however long it takes you to play the course of events out in your head, or to talk to someone to do it for you. The end result is almost never as you suspect, and Renée Zellweger doesn't work at your office if you have to leave. You probably don't even have an aquarium.

Verbal misdemeanors, on the other hand, are much harder to control. If you're not careful, you can say what you really think before you realize you've really thought it. And after you've really said it, well, now you've really done it.

Is That a Size Twelve in Your Mouth?

"There is no man, however wise, who has not at some period of his youth said things...he would gladly, if he could, expunge it from his memory."

—Marcel Proust, prolific French author who showed little evidence of ever expunging anything

Managers and seniors can get away with shooting from the hip a little bit, because they've earned it. They've got credibility, and a history of getting things right, and would probably go to work for a competitor and make your life more difficult if you fired them. But you've got less wiggle room than coach class on United Airlines.

Practically everything passing through your lips at the entry level is a strike either for or against your professional judgment. Which you don't really have any of yet. So do shut up—especially during sensitive meetings and catty gossip sessions with fellow grunts. Remember, if this person works with you today, they're still going to work with you tomorrow. Except now whatever you've said has the potential to get back to them, which you're nearly guaranteed of if it's your boss. Rather, just smile and curse under your breath, like the rest of us.

Keep in mind, what you may consider to be an acceptable protest or deserved criticism, the company may see as attitude or insubordination. It's not until after many months of watching folks voice up that you'll understand what's on- and off-limits. Plus people don't always know themselves until they try it. So, when in doubt, just say nothing and appear stupid. Better that than to speak and have them know for sure.

> " Knowing when to keep your mouth shut is invariably more important than opening it at the right time. "
>
> —Publisher Malcolm Forbes, who was better at the second one

P eople hate politicians. Even politicians don't like politicians, and not only when they're smearing each other on TV. You're always wondering about their motives and sincerity and which lobbyists and interns they're lying about getting "contributions" from.

Which is the first of three reasons why you need to be nonpartisan and easygoing and someone your coworker can confide in about the salary chart they found over in accounting. There's no more reliable way to stay up on the dirt—often the profitable kind—than by being someone who people feel comfortable telling things they really shouldn't be. Remember, it's always good to be liked, and it's especially good to be liked at the entry level.

Second, managers all want employees who put in a solid day's work without running their mouths off. It makes the team so much easier to handle, and usually means he gets to go

> 66 Politics is perhaps the only profession for which no preparation is thought necessary. 99
>
> —Robert Louis Stevenson, who forgot about parenthood

home earlier, which you're all going to benefit from. So avoid taking unpopular positions—even the ones you really agree with—or mingling very closely with those who do (as in bad brand associations).

> **For every complex problem, there is a simple solution that is elegant, easy to understand, and wrong.**
>
> —H. L. Mencken, explaining my college grades in calculus

And if you feel like a sellout for not speaking up...good, you should, because that's exactly what you are. Your manager is, too. And by selling out together, you'll get promoted and earn enough money and experience to go do something you feel better about. Remember, it's always good to be respected, and it's especially good to be respected by your entry level boss.

Third, for whatever political understanding you do amass, it's still not enough. Not even close. The machinations of your company are very much a *Wizard of Oz,* man-behind-the-curtain sort of thing, and you never know what levers and buttons are being worked back there. Remember, it's always bad to get into political trouble, and it's especially bad to get into political trouble at

how do you play politics?

There ain't no answer.

There ain't going to be any answer.

There has never been an answer.

That's the answer.

—Gertrude Stein

the entry level. You don't have the pull yet to get yourself out, and a boss with the same issue as the Scarecrow.

Get Enlightened

Michael and Deborah Dobson, in their book *Enlightened Office Politics* (as if there's anything less fit for enlightenment), define politics as:

"The informal and sometimes emotion-driven process of allocating limited resources and working out goals, decisions, and actions in an environment of people with different and competing interests and personalities." (They should warn you to take a breath before reading that.)

Translated, this says that everybody wants the big piece of pie, and they're going to fight you for it. So what do they recommend?

- Being principled and honest
- Committing to company goals
- Showing respect for opinions

This is a little fluffy, I grant you. But they've got a point with the respect bit: You've always got to be agreeable about how you disagree. There are a lot of ways to tell somebody they're full of shit, after all, and still be able to have a beer with them after work.

Lie no. 44
To Get What You Want,
Do What You Have To

The cutthroat thing only works in college classes, professional sports, and divorce settlements. At the office, instead, it's all about catching the flies with honey; or, more commonly, just letting them buzz around and annoy the piss out of you.

Newbies typically take two routes with their unchecked ambition: going over heads and stepping on toes. More specifically, their *manager's* head and toes—both of which he can, and probably will, subsequently use in tandem to make your pooper hurt when you sit down.

Similar to when the company asks you to come in on a weekend, grunts don't take no for an answer very well. Especially when they confuse the issue of their dissatisfaction with anybody else's. So, sure enough, you'll find them calling hush-hush meetings with people they shouldn't be (i.e., their boss's boss, other managers, HR), asking for

> **There are no personal sympathies in politics.**
>
> —First female British Prime minister Margaret Thatcher, who, unfortunately for him, took the same stance with her husband

things they have no business asking for (i.e., getting them to do what their manager already said he wouldn't), and agreeing to take on work he never approved (i.e., the kind you don't mind staying awake for). Except at this point you've just created about half a dozen different conflicts of interest. Including, shortly, between you and your landlord, because the unemployment check won't cover rent.

As we've already decided, your boss is your demigod. He may let bad things happen to good people (i.e., you), but you've got to have faith that there's some kind of plan out there, much too big for you to understand. It's this sort of reasoning, I know, that leads to atheism and Scientology and whatever else Hollywood's into this week. But being a believer at the entry level, I promise, will get you saved. Or at least a recommendation, when you need it, for a better job.

Once more, your manager is accounting for political issues you have no conception of when he puts the kibosh on one of your requests or initiatives. That said, he's also got his own interests in keeping other managers happy when they want to use you, so sometimes there's a middle ground to be negotiated. Regardless, the receipt for your labor is sitting in his drawer, so he can do pretty much whatever the hell he wants (or doesn't want), and it's tough luck if you don't like it. Or him. Which is about all the luck most career freshmen get.

Moreover, you've got to keep an eye on any other toes that might be jutting out. If you want to carve out a niche in market research, to continue our example, you're probably doing so at the expense of someone who's doing a marginal job with it right now. If they're a fellow grunt, screw 'em, you're both fighting for the same spot (which still isn't an exception to the "honey" rule, because you're going to do it with a big, aggravating smile). But if it's a vet, give them the chance to save face and spin it as "assistance" or "a great learning opportunity," and then you both win. As, incidentally, does the company.

> ### Like Men Do during the First Few Dates
>
> "Under certain conditions one yields a city, sacrifices a portion of his force, or gives up ground in order to gain a more valuable objective."
>
> —Sun Tzu, from *The Art of War,* the world's oldest, most over-adapted military treatise (including for cooking)

Which, never forget, isn't yours to fix. It just confuses management when you try.

Y ou can always tell who's got nothing to do: They're making the rounds with all the cubes they know, chitchatting and interrupting workflow, sending distracting email links to random articles and other crap they found on the Web, disappearing for a good two, three hours in the middle of the day. It's welcome if you, yourself, don't really have much on your plate (buzzword-a-rama!), or if I've just described your typical day. But this gets old pretty quickly, and it's not like your boss is oblivious to all the places you're getting your office passport stamped.

Sitting on your thumb, once in a while, is okay; it's expected, even, at the end of a long project—kind of your "decompression time." (Unless you're really at a burn-and-churn organization, in which case you would've heard about it the first time you got caught taking one of those online astrological compatibility quizzes.) And not that we don't all, from time to time, randomly shuffle stacks of paper from one side of the desk to the other. Or stroke our chin over some imposing 11" x 17" spreadsheet we lifted from the copy room. Or, most typically, just let the eyes glaze on whatever program's unaccountably up on the screen. But that's not convincing anyone when month-end chargeability numbers are being crunched. And it's certainly not convincing the boss of your ambition or efficiency or ability to sell BS.

Not to say that you run up to your manager the second you've finished an assignment and ask for something else (no "over-delivering" there, and you don't want it to look like you need your nose wiped). Rather, this is about recognizing that, even if you're not explicitly tasked, the company still owns every moment of your day while you're using their electricity. So if you've got some time on your hands—after paying bills and making dinner reservations and finishing up all of your personal emails, of course—put it to work on an initiative that's going to benefit both you and the business.

We'll spend the rest of the chapter talking about the ins-and-outs of doing this, but note first that it has to come after whatever work the company can actually issue an invoice for. No matter how much this extra project may excite you or showcase your brains or rub your soft little elbows with the guys who drive BMWs, it's not going to play if it's at the expense of you typing and distributing those meeting minutes. Never forget, you're a grunt before anything else. Because you absolutely don't want them reminding you.

The only time you've ever had the best ideas is maybe in bed, with someone much younger than you and easily impressed. Otherwise, when you've really crinkled foreheads, it was probably the result of you stealing something. And, just like with your college term papers, "intellectual capital" is pickpocketed all the time around the workplace. Except now there's no suspicious, semi-retired professor checking your bibliography because he's got nothing better to do with his tenure.

Old folks, in fact, are the best ones to lift insights from, because they've been around long enough to know what the good ideas are. Then why haven't they pushed these though and taken credit themselves, you ask? Same reason nobody before them did: It's easy to bitch about a problem, but an even bigger bitch to actually do something about it. So most people just play dead when it comes to taking on new work, or trying to fix a

> " We don't need men with new ideas as much as we need men who will put energy behind the old ones. "
>
> —William Feather, who read your manager's mind exactly

problem that they're not getting paid to fix. Even major irritations and headaches—stuff you'd totally get pills or a cream for if it were your body—are tolerated, worked around, and fought through until the next time. So you're going to be a better burglar than they ever were, and make off with the smarts of someone who was stupid enough to be talking before doing.

"Wouldn't it be great if..." "You know, what we really need is..." "I once tried to..." Listen carefully to comments that start something like this, including for blackmail purposes, and see how doable and relevant the proposal is—which are the two big hooks here: Can you pull this off, and will the organization actually care that you did?

The first order of business, then, is determining if this scheme is even workable, both tactically and politically. As we'll chat about a little later, plenty of good ideas get wasted on bad management, so you need to ask about what's been pitched and pooh-poohed before you got there. You also have to make sure that you don't get carried away and dilute your efforts here with a bunch of different initiatives. Just choose one really good one, and then work the hell out of it. Like a niche or a pickup line.

> 66 **If at first you don't succeed, destroy all evidence that you tried.** 99
>
> —Susan Ohanian, who would've fit in just fine on the Enron accounting team

The second part is figuring out if this project makes sense for the business, as far as you understand it. And the great thing about nicking outside ideas is that you don't really have to know entirely how the industry and company work, just this little part of it. As a general rule, though—and one of the most important you'll ever learn—follow the money trail to determine what's going to be compelling to management. (There's an old saying that goes, "The answer to 90 percent of all questions is *money*." And the company wants that up to 93 percent by the end of the quarter.)

So stuff like community activities and social events—team-building retreats, canned food drives, and the like—may make you feel all cozy and popular, but they're not going to get the attention of anyone who's going to give you a raise. Keep the volunteer work outside of the office, and focus instead on cutting costs and improving performance. At this point, *you're* really the charity in need of donations.

> " All the really good ideas I ever had came to me while I was milking a cow. "
>
> —Grant Wood (with no point to this one, but I couldn't resist)

Lie no. 47
Good Ideas Sell Themselves

Even though they gave you a desk and a phone and let you send inappropriate emails from an "@company.com" address, the assumption remains that you can find your way to offsite meetings, but not much past that. If even that.

Which isn't completely your fault: Most organizations that do any training at all—especially rare at places with a few hundred FTEs or less ("full-time employees," which I think counts as a buzzword with HR)—typically limit it to the immediate functions of your job. Makes sense from a downtime and cost perspective; makes no sense from anywhere else you're standing. Except, maybe, when it's in a competitor's lobby with your résumé.

> **The power of an idea can be measured by the degree of resistance it attracts.**
>
> —David Yoho, who later decided the same thing about his cologne

Regardless, this is one of the places where that personal syllabus of yours gets uncrumpled. To get anything of personal interest done at the entry level, you've got to pitch it in a way that appeals to the heart and soul of any enterprise: the pocketbook. Even when it's a matter of personal conflict, the company's main interest is that it doesn't affect quality, productivity, morale, or client satisfaction—all of which have a currency conversion. So no matter what it is that you want to accomplish, it has to demonstrably grow the business to get the green light. And you've got to prove it with, like, numbers.

Again, when it comes to grasping the company's business model and financial workings, you're believed to be just short of needing a wet nurse and an after-lunch nap—which you may already take, eyes closed or not. So it'll be a real stunner if you can approach them like a seasoned pro, and call out step-by-step how you see your scheme impacting the operations of your group or

The Business Case

Got a big idea to knock 'em on their backside? Better be ready to prove it can do at least one of these:

- Help the company save money
- Help the company make money
- Help your manager look like a pimp

And stuff like this (or "metrics," if you want to sound like you mean it) is what makes their ears perk up:

- Faster turnaround times/more efficient processes
- Fewer errors/better QA
- Improved work product/happier clients
- Wider margins (lower costs/higher revenue)
- Strengthened communications/team morale
- Potential downside/risk management
- Why your boss will get praised/promoted/improved self-esteem

Remember to leave emotion out of it; this isn't personal to anyone but you and your precious little ego.

Authors note: You have to subtly imply that last bullet; being too explicit about it will make you look like a suck-up, which you have to pretend you're not. (But you are.) (And should be.)

department in a meaningful and relevant way. (Same thing works great with parents, by the way.)

> ❝ **To get your ideas across, use small words, big ideas, and short sentences.** ❞
>
> —John Henry Patterson (with the addendum that today you need to tack on, "in PowerPoint")

But do be quick and to the point about it. Smart ideas can sound plenty dumb when they're not articulated well, so maybe do the PowerPoint thing for your high-level sales job—*concisely,* for a busy executive, which your manager isn't, but likes to imagine he is. (Bank of America, for instance, allows no more than two fonts and seven lines per slide, to avoid the "ransom note look," as NPR commentator Geoff Nunberg puts it.) Hard data comes later, and it does come. Done right, however, your idea might, too…

But I wouldn't bet any grocery money on it.

Lie no. 48
Politics Don't Affect Good Ideas

After looking around your company for a while and scratching your head, you can probably pick out a dozen and a half things straight off the bat that should be working differently. And for all of your greenness, chances are you're noticing good stuff.

Now all you have to do is scribble down the hundred-plus other line items to fix, figure out how to actually fix them, and then get the right people on board to champion all of that refreshing change through the system. And when you're done with that, we're going to need you to go to the Middle East and get everyone to stop shooting each other, if you can block out the time on your calendar.

I'm not saying getting new ideas going is impossible—it's the *people* who are. Everybody knows what's broken around the place, but it really doesn't matter how well things are going; what matters is who it's keeping happy. If the powers that be like it, then it works. Whether or not it really does. At all.

> " The only thing that can overcome a persuasive idea is a better idea. "
>
> —Theodore Repplier, who discounts managers and wives

Mind the Gap

"Before you start yelling about how things need to be changed, you have to understand the culture," warns Don Fisher, founder of hip clothier and carefree commercial-maker Gap, Inc. "Don't arrive and think you know everything." (Recurring theme, huh?)

As we've touched on, you may have a dazzling initiative that's already been tried and failed miserably. Just because you've seen it or heard about it working somewhere else doesn't mean that the culture of this particular organization is going to support the idea.

Remember, every company—like every love affair—is different. What works in one relationship doesn't necessarily work in another. Which is also why you need accounts at both Victoria's Secret and Trashy Lingerie.

So you need to be aware of the histories behind certain customs and conventions around the office, and figure out if this particular issue is something you can step around. Even compelling business cases lose nine out of ten times to ego and tradition—and if you think you know the answer, management has that many more years on you of thinking the very same thing. And being right more often.

The tack, instead, isn't to fight the system, but rather to work within its constraints to try to push your agenda through. (And by agenda, I mean the one—at the most two—things per year you want to have a conversation about.) And even then, your discussion will probably remain just that.

Corporate receptiveness to new stuff is a function of just the right idea, tossed out at just the right time, and presented in just the right way (i.e., just the right business case, touching on just the right issues, endorsed by just the right people). Then your manager has to decide if your analysis was accurate, decide how he personally feels about it, decide how much time he has to put behind it, decide what priority it has to the group, and finally decide how hard it will be to convince the people who need convincing. Which, after reading this paragraph, probably now includes you.

It shouldn't, though. Yes, you're going to lose nearly every time; but people come and go nearly as often, and bring all of their loopy perspectives with them. So what may have been beaten up by

No Means No

"Oh, would that my mind could let fall its dead ideas, as the tree does with its withered leaves!"

—André Gide

one boss might very well be embraced by another. Plus the business environment is worse than an adolescent girl when it comes to changing tastes, so sometimes your idea will finally make sense from the outside in. Provided "sense" is one of the things your company happens to make.

Lie no. 49
Ideas Are as Good When Coming from You

I deas, oftentimes, are only as credible as the mouth they come out of. Which is especially regrettable when you listen to some of the fabulously stupid suggestions by senior staff that get seriously kicked around. Meanwhile you're back here streamlining operations and identifying seven-figure opportunities in Hong Kong. Or at least you're right on top of it when they run out of binder clips.

What's worse is when you come up with an idea that's a non-starter, and then watch someone a couple of levels above you start the damn thing right up. Unfortunately, though, that's just the way it happens at the bottom, so be careful with who knows what you're thinking. Except your boss, who may end up lifting the suggestion himself, and that's fine—your thoughts are his when they're any good, and it's actually a pretty big compliment. Besides, it just means he's more likely to go to bat for you when raises and bonuses are being worked

> 66 That fellow seems to me to possess but one idea, and that a wrong one. 99

—Samuel Johnson, who wasn't talking about your boss, much as it may apply

out at the end of the year (so then he can really put the screws to you when he needs some smart thinking in a hurry).

And the point of coming up with clever ideas isn't really to watch them come to life—it's just to show that you can come up with clever ideas. See, to do your job well is one thing; to show that you're thinking critically about the company's business, now that's quite another. Your manager hasn't even got that down.

It's the difference between being told what to do, and being able to tell them what should be done (since you're the one actually doing it). Not that you're necessarily going to nail it, or that it's going to be politically feasible; but the speaking up demonstrates that you have an eye for the bigger picture. So if you're

Ideas in the Mist

Peter Gruber, chairman of Mandalay Entertainment, regales us with a story about their 1988 film *Gorillas in the Mist*. (You know, the one where that hippie anthropologist hangs out in the jungle, and writes down which ape picks ticks out of the other's fur and whatnot.)

After they bought the rights to the picture and were starting to shoot, it dawned on them that the script called for the gorillas to actually "act." And while that hasn't stopped anyone else in Hollywood, they nonetheless called an emergency meeting to figure out what they were going to do.

Turns out they let a young intern sit in on the discussion (to take notes or make coffee, I'm sure), who, after a while, meekly suggested, "What if you let the gorillas write the story?" In other words, send a cinematographer into the habitat with a bunch of film, and then wrap the picture around whatever you get.

After laughing her out of the room—but not coming up with anything better than sticking actors in ape suits—they actually went with the girl's proposal. The result: phenomenal footage that wrote the story for them, a film shot for half of the original $40 million budget, and a Golden Globe for Sigourney Weaver. Bet you the coffee was tasty, too.

wrong, you're wrong. And if you're right, your boss is a freakin' genius for thinking of that. Aren't you lucky to have him?

.   .   .   .

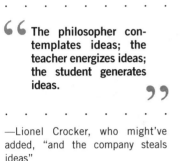 The philosopher contemplates ideas; the teacher energizes ideas; the student generates ideas.

.   .   .   .

—Lionel Crocker, who might've added, "and the company steals ideas"

Lie no. 50
You Can Sleep with Your Coworkers

You've heard the sayings: "Don't fish off the company pier"; "Don't dip your pen into corporate ink"; "Steal Post-Its, not…" Take your pick, they're all dead on.

I mean, when things go bad with most anyone else in your world (even family and friends), you can usually make the decision not to deal with them anymore, much less five days a week. But should a workplace romance turn sour, you're stuck interacting—or at least maintaining bumping-into distance—with this person for the duration of your or their employment. Which doesn't sound nearly as intimidating until you've actually had to share an elevator or group project with someone who's yelled at you naked.

So you have to do an exceptionally careful cost-benefit analysis before you go trading orgasms with a colleague. It can be hard to avoid, I know, when you're spending ten or twelve hours a day laboring side-by-side, eating take-out in

> " See, the problem is that God gives men a brain and a penis, and only enough blood to run one at a time. "
>
> —Robin Williams, summarizing one of the meanest jokes in the history of man

Cupid in the Cubicle

According to Vault.com's 2005 Office Romance Survey, 58 percent of employees say they've been involved in a workplace love affair—up by about 12 percent from the year earlier. And check out everyone else mixing business with pleasure:

- Successfully kept their relationship a secret 26%
- Have hooked up in the office (bathroom, conference room, etc.) 23%
- Met their spouse on the job 22%
- Boss dated an employee 19%
- Company policy saying bosses can't date their employees 17%

the office at ten o'clock, and sharing those "how sad are *we*"-type conversations. Quietly that turns into backrubs—just to relieve the stress, you know—some playful little banter, and maybe a little footsy under the desk. Then, of course, you're ripping each other's clothes off and having hot, wild monkey sex in the one conference room that has a lock on the door.

Sure, once in a while we hear about how so-and-so met their spouse at the office, and hey, check out the wedding photos on the company intranet. But most of the time people just break up, leaving all of that gossip and tension to deal with. And then not only does work quality suffer because you can't concentrate—which doesn't exactly bode well for that promotion, or even keeping the job you've got—but it inhibits the kind of breathing room any sexual relationship needs to keep properly aerated. Should you stay together and not end up eviscerating one another in meetings.

But your boss still might: He could choose, at his whim, to impose a transfer or pass you over for the marquee projects—believing your head is elsewhere, or that you're indiscreet, or that it should've been him. Plus just think if one of you were promoted into a reporting relationship (especially her): Not only would it poison the working environment—particularly if she starts earning more, because we all know how well men deal with *that*—but you'd also probably lose your enthusiasm for some of the master-and-servant games back home.

So, in short, make sure he or she has a real shot at being The One if you're going to go for it. I'll be the first one to say sacrifice anything and everything for a chance at real, true love. But the sex is never worth the divisiveness a scorned lover can cause when you mix faxing with… Anyway.

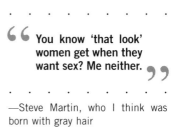

> **You know 'that look' women get when they want sex? Me neither.**
>
> —Steve Martin, who I think was born with gray hair

I guess the big message I'm trying to put out there with all this, really—the one I want you to take home with you and not forget—is to, please, make sure your résumé is always current.

66 **Women need a reason
to have sex. Men just
need a place.** 99

—Billy Crystal, except not in the
copy room. Never in the copy room.

It's Up or Out

Lie no. 51
Promotions Are Based on Hard Work

Say you're the fastest one in your group, banging out projects like one of those sweatshop kids in Thailand, who might lose a finger if they didn't. Sooner rather than later, your manager is going to run out of work to give you, and then you become one of those accidental tourists we talked about. Meanwhile, your screw-off coworkers are buffering their usability numbers—nearly going at an English-as-a-second-language pace. So as profit-per-employee is tabulated when the books are being reviewed, you're actually going to come in below the guy who typically spends his afternoons on illegal Internet downloads and aggressive coffee and cigarette breaks.

Friends Lead to High Places

"He who would rise in the world should veil his ambitions with the forms of humanity."

—Chinese proverb

In short, promotions aren't based on hard work; they're based on the *perception* of hard work. Not that you can create the illusion without actually doing a fair amount of it, but you've got to be a little strategic about how and when you do. Which includes, one, managing your *delivery;* and two, managing your *documentation.*

Which ultimately means managing your *impressions*—how people collectively regard you and your work around the office. Assuming, first, they could actually pick you out of a lineup.

Over-delivery we've already hashed out, and the other two we'll continue in a minute. What we need to talk about here is sitting on stuff for a while. It sounds completely counterintuitive, but there's definitely such a thing as being too efficient. And it'll lead to one of three outcomes: too much work, not enough work, or expectations that you can't (or don't want to) meet.

Your company, like many of the ex's we've dated, is a taker: It figures out what it can juice you for, and then gets to squeezing. Which

$\sum_\Theta^2$ **Entry Level Math** ∞
$a\beta$

With all the spam about how to make things bigger, it's a shame there's nothing about cubes. So if you want to have the company moan with delight, your business case has to show:

- What you made faster, cheaper, or better—and with what results
- How much more you sold or delivered (in dollars)
- Which milestones you hit and passed, including vs. peers
- Why they'll love you long time $\geq \Delta$

means hard work usually just leads to more hard work—and no more money. Sure, this will get you promoted eventually, but it sets a bad precedent. You'll always have to bend it like Beckham to accommodate, and it's not so easy to break up this time.

Otherwise, blowing through your deadlines can kill your chargeability numbers (at least at professional services organizations). You might mitigate the effect, of course, by keeping tight with your boss, but he's still got to show his stats to his own superiors. So if there's not enough work to go around, not only are you bored, but you're making your manager worry about keeping you busy—which he's worried enough about for himself.

> ❝ **A work of real merit finds favor at last.** ❞
>
> —Amos Bronson Alcott, who's obviously never worked in publishing

Expectations are also cumulative, meaning if you do that project fast, you should be able to do this one just as quickly. Maybe you can, maybe you can't, but that's the wrong way to go into an assignment. It leaves little or no room for upside surprise, and puts you under the gun to perform (and cancel dates you worked even harder to get).

So beat your peer group by a day instead of a week, and invest the downtime into a good initiative. I've seldom seen one of those turned in late.

Promotions are about politics, and politics are about people. So, if my math is right, promotions are really about people—and politics is actually about money. Which, of course, is about power. Hence, your need for influential friends with liberal expense accounts.

How far you go in an organization is absolutely contingent upon how strong your connections are with the players: your manager, other managers, senior colleagues, Midases, mentors, influential peers, any execs who know your name for some reason. Hitting your targets and running spellcheck and keeping your foot out of your mouth during meetings are just the baseline; that only means you haven't taken yourself out of contention. (And even then you've got a shot, as evidenced by some of the mental giants sporting a

I'm with Him...

Research cited by new-age biz magazine *Fast Company* shows that in over 80 percent of promotions, candidates have a relationship with someone higher up in the food chain who speaks out on their behalf.

The other 20 percent move up because the outside candidates are too expensive, or their résumés suggest dyslexia.

Author's note: Second paragraph is my research, which your HR rep will gladly confirm for you.

fatter title than you.) No, the real decision is made by who's going to bat for you. Or by who's trying to toss you from the game.

We already know how important it is to be cool with your boss, especially heading into performance review season. But you also have to account for all of your other relationships, which can sometimes pull just as much weight, if not more. Make friends with a respected manager or VP, for instance, and he might be able to help veto any dissenting votes below him. Piss off a senior confidante of your boss, conversely, and she's going to give him a laundry list of everything you've made a mistake even *thinking* about.

So if you need to get couples counseling with anyone who might have your manager's ear, go do it before bonuses hit the calculator. It's not an overnight thing, obviously—and if you come out of nowhere, the ploy

---

DIGJAM File

Acronym

"Damn I'm Good, Just Ask Me."

Usage

To support your business case for a promotion or raise during performance reviews. Match up each claim of greatness with a solid piece of data.

Purpose

B/C companies forget when it's too expensive to remember

Contents

- "Good Work!" emails from important people
- Samples from successful projects
- Documentation of issues you helped to fix
- Hard data about what you improved, and how it's impacted the business
- Arguments for questions and objections, like why your gross pay is so gross

might backfire—so just very subtly start saying good morning, or offering to lend a hand, or at least quit stealing things from their desk at night. Doesn't mean, either, that you start up with the girl-talk bit, or make it some big come-on. You just need them not to loathe you to the extent that they might slam you when it counts.

And don't go slinging mud yourself. Especially if it's a peer, and you're both vying for the same spot. Undercutting doesn't work at the office (at least not at your level), and you're not going to change management's mind—except maybe in the other direction. They'll pick the candidate they like better before the more qualified one, and then spend the money on training. Plus I'd hate to be you if they make this guy your senior.

> 66 I don't care what is written about me so long as it isn't true. 99

—Katharine Hepburn, who would've failed miserably in an office if acting hadn't worked out

Lie no. 53
You'll Get Promoted During a Bad Stretch

This isn't one you can do so much about, but rather just become aware of. Like being gay.

We already know the company is on par with your local retirement community in the long-term memory department, and that your standing in the organization is very much a "what have you photocopied for me lately?" kind of thing. Now, as it pertains to you being promoted, if they're not very happy with you tonight, you can forget about getting lucky.

The most important intangible factor in any promotion: *momentum.* True everywhere, you want to ask for something—especially a big something—when the giver is feeling all good about you and life and, ideally, has a BAC above .08.

In approaching your boss with a random issue, you can usually wait him out until one of those Fridays where people start sneaking out around two o'clock. But with performance reviews, it's ready or not, here they come. So if you happen to be in the tank this month, the discussion's not waiting until you can smooth things

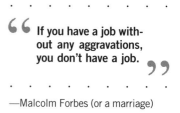

> **If you have a job without any aggravations, you don't have a job.**
>
> —Malcolm Forbes (or a marriage)

over with some weekend work, or a yummy vanilla latté for my favorite boss. Delish!

Yet what you can do is to start stepping it up just before you're scheduled to sit down. Maybe it means letting your manager see you clicking away at the keyboard on his way out—and again on his way in, if you can safely bathe and dress yourself at that hour. Or perhaps this is the point when you bring up that initiative you've been chewing on, and hey, how does he think it'll work for the team? (Which, by the way, you see some great opportunities for.) And, sorry, would it be all right if you took on some overflow work for so-and-so, because they seem a little overwhelmed right now.

Basically, blind him with all the sunshine coming out of your ass, and make sure the rest of you is dripping with success. Along with, maybe, some sweat from that second coat of wax on his Lexus.

Got Paycheck?

According to a recent study by CareerBuilder.com, 53 percent of men are unhappy with their salary—a 23 percent jump from those who said so in 2001.

One out of two women are also dissatisfied with their take-home, which has remained constant over the past few years.

So, basically, half of all employees are pissed over pay. And they say there's no equality in the workplace.

Annual Reviews

Peter Goodman, in his book *Win-Win Career Negotiations* (both wins are for the company, I think), outlines what he sees as the six main points of a good annual review. I've basically already said the same things, but maybe you need a second opinion:

- Record all of your accomplishments throughout the year.

- Illustrate your successes: "Your boss is likely to remember only things that have happened over the past month."

- See yourself in partnership with your manager. (Interpret that one however you like.)

- Go in with an open mind: "If you view criticism as constructive, you will be more apt to listen." And not hit him.

- Focus on mutual accountability, not money.

- Empower yourself: "Stand up for yourself in terms of the input you need from your manager" (e.g., stapled or paperclipped).

Fortune 500 companies are funny like this: They'll sit their grunts down when they first arrive, and map out the next dozen or so years of their life there. Knowing full well that most will be gone in under two. And that their interests are going to shift over time. And that many aren't even good enough to hang. And that execs hardly ever follow the prescribed career path, anyway. But let me tell you again about all the exciting stuff you'll be doing in 2012.

No, the best kind of promotion, arguably, is into a position that wasn't a position before you got it. Or, more accurately, before you *earned* it, which is how it works regardless of where and how you move; (almost) no matter what, you have to already be doing the job before you officially get the job. (The hedge is for when they shove you into a manager role—supervising people doing the work you did so well, they decided to have you stop doing it.)

> 66 **Anyone can do any amount of work, provided it isn't the work he is supposed to be doing at that moment.** 99
>
> —Robert Benchley, explaining why it's so hard to get the trash taken out

As we've talked about, corporations have some heavy ADD when it comes to strategy, and most are willing to throw a few bucks at the Next Big Thing. So what you need to be doing is dolling yourself up for the gig—really working your niche, and keeping abreast of all the goings-on in the company and industry. You might yet be able to yank a better business card out of it if you can make a strong enough pitch for the new post. And also refill their Ritalin prescription.

Actually getting a job classified on the books, however, is no trivial matter. It usually involves salary structure adjustments and divisional slotting and a bunch of other technical HR crap. Meaning your business case, this time, is really going to have to get your manager all riled up, and give him some numbers to throw at his bosses. Real ones, I mean; from credible sources. Published this year. Without rounding up.

So, as you guessed, many times the organization won't support a full-time staff position, and that's fine. If it's something that's adding value to the company, you'll be recognized one way or the other. Plus in the meantime, you'll be building unique skill sets in differentiated and highly marketable areas, which you can leverage as you transition into a

> 66 **God gives every bird his food, but he does not throw it into the nest.** 99
>
> —Josiah Holland, commenting on why they've got wings and you've got a commute

best-fit career opportunity. (Wow, sorry, had a management consulting flashback there.)

Regular, organic, or with cheese, however, make sure you really want this promotion before you make a run at it. I've seen too many grunts get caught up in the glitz and glamour of moving up in the ranks, only to find themselves in a job they don't like much more than their old one. Oftentimes less, what with the additional hours and expectations and headaches. Plus the paycheck is a sock-in-the-jock deal: much bigger from the outside, until you pull out all the taxes.

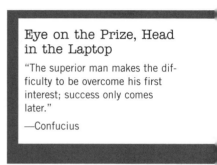

Eye on the Prize, Head in the Laptop

"The superior man makes the difficulty to be overcome his first interest; success only comes later."

—Confucius

We'll spend the better part of the last four chapters discussing the ins and outs of finding the work you love. But until you get there, you've got to think through what you want your day-to-day to look like—if this isn't something that might just look better on the mannequin in the store window. You never want your career path, after all, to be the result of blind ambition or desperate escape. That's for dating.

Lie no. 55
Transfers Aren't as Good as Promotions

Accepting a promotion you don't really want is just getting more of something you don't really like. Um…except money. But even then, it's not like you'll have much time to spend it. Or anyone, most likely, to spend it on. Unless you count Jim Beam and Captain Morgan as "friends."

And you don't have to quit, either, to go mingle with a new crowd. Rather, one of the great things about working at a big company—if that's where you work— is all of the different divisions and groups who like to think the place wouldn't run without them. So if things aren't working out back home as you thought they would, or if you're exposed to an area of the business you get excited about, what's stopping you from hooking-up down the hall?

Don't Make This Mistake Twice

"You have got to know what it is that you want, or someone is going to sell you a bill of goods along the line."

—Richard Nelson Bolles, from *What Color is Your Parachute?*

Your manager or the company might be stopping you, actually, but we'll put that aside for the moment. The point here is that taking off or taking a bad promotion aren't necessarily your only two options when you hit a wall with your career. Transfers, instead, can reinvigorate you professionally, get you off of Zoloft, and offer you yet another way to go make a mess of things as you learn on the company's tab.

If it's a dramatic switch—say, from finance into creative, or some 180-degree turn like that—you probably won't be walking into the same kind of money or title you were pulling with the 10-key. But if you happen to have game, you should also happen to move up that much more quickly. And the real point is that you enjoy it, which makes this one of the best alternatives to denting

your résumé or credibility as you Forrest Gump it through your old department.

Especially consider rolling your chair over if it means sharing cube space with smarter people. You can learn plenty from your assignments (e.g., which coffee filter leaves the fewest grounds in the carafe), but nowhere near what you can shake out of the heads of rock star managers: Listening to them talk, thinking in new ways, drawing from their energy and excitement, rising to the level of play—that's where you'll really start to grow and be challenged and have some fun. Plus these are the folks who are going to stay with you throughout your career, and drag you up with them.

So get a bead on what else is happening in your organization, and who you need to start talking with to potentially move over. But not in terms of a full-blown position straight away; that scares off people in bars *and* in cubes. Rather, just poke around for something small you can open up with. Then if they like you, they'll buy you a drink. (Ah, friends…)

Send Him to Voicemail

"Even though you might be offered a good position," warns Bob Cohn, former CEO of both Lucent and Octel Technologies, "if it's for a bunch of loose cannons who don't know what they're doing, you will make a lot of mistakes and won't learn much from them." (Sound like anyone you might report to?)

Along with the engineering brains of the operation, Peter Olsen, Cohn found his way into voicemail—otherwise a bad thing—and built one of the most widely adopted systems around.

"If you work for the right people, however, they will teach you well," Bob continues. "You'll then have the right values and skill sets." You'll also have someone who doesn't blow smoke or give you a blank stare when you ask a hard question.

—Quotes from *How They Achieved*

Lie no. 56
Politically, Transfers Are No Problem

Just as promotions are a political animal, transfers are too. Maybe even more so, because it involves cooperation and egos between departments—and isn't as typical and "clean" as just hoisting someone up beyond their capabilities, and giving them another $10K a year to mess up their direct reports' lives.

And the first issue at hand is, of course, money: Headcounts are hard to come by (more HR mumbo-jumbo for how many people at what level are in the budget). Meaning even if you and this group are all over each other, they first have to have the cash sitting around to pay your salary. Then they need to come up with enough work to actually cover that salary, and still turn a decent profit on the deal. Which also isn't going to happen if you've got a would-be boss who's in the doghouse with senior management, or if the company is shifting emphasis away from this particular department.

So let's say you take care of all that. Now you've

> **Wherever there is a man who exercises authority, there is a man who resists authority.**
>
> —Oscar Wilde, summing up my teenage years

got to compete against the people who made up their mind to do this sort of work long before you did, and have the résumés to prove it. Which still doesn't take you out of the running. Far from it, in fact, as being on the inside confers one of the best advantages possible when it comes to moving up and around. (Many firms even have a stated objective of "promoting from within" if you look at their public relations documents. Never mind that it saves thousands of dollars on recruiting and training, and makes employees feel like they've got a fighting chance at being able to afford a mortgage one day if they hang around long enough.)

> ❝ **If you want to make enemies, try to change something.** ❞
>
> —Woodrow Wilson, who said this even before TV remotes were invented

Okay, so we've got a hiring manager who's not entirely horror-struck at the idea of you sitting near him, and a heap of outside candidates who couldn't manage to spell the company name correctly in their cover letters. No matter how promising things look, assume it's not going to happen. Which isn't being pessimistic—just practical. Realistic, frankly, given all of the sensitivities and personalities and parts of the mousetrap that have to click just right. Even the best of intentions often lead to a whole lot of nothing, and you can't count on someone spending too much of their political capital on some newbie they're doing a favor for. And a risky favor at that.

Fine, settled, it's still moving forward. Now, if there were ever a time to "shut your pie hole," as dead comedian Chris Farley so eloquently put it, this is that time. Hell, if you even have a restless night's dream about letting one of your coworkers in on it, you need to punch yourself in the face very hard after you wake up. Twice.

Go blabbing, and you'll be in your boss's guest chair by day's end, guaranteed. Not that he isn't going to be one of the big dealmakers in this trade, but it's all about timing: Should he find out you've been sniffing around another department and you don't have anything solid lined up, you're stuck reporting to a guy who knows (for sure now) you don't want to be reporting to him. And even if the transfer does magically go through at this point, you'll probably still be touching his group somehow. Which is going to hurt.

Experienced managers don't take this kind of thing personally—especially from grunts. The standing bet, however, is that your boss isn't one of those people. So make the story about you and your growing interests, and not him and his growing incompetence.

> " Since a politician never believes what he says, he is surprised when others believe him. "
>
> —Charles de Gaulle (and same for Don King)

Lie no. 57
Up Is the Only Way Out

Few careers go straight up anymore, now that the corporate ladder is firewood (more on that later). These days, instead, there's usually some give and take to it—you know, one step forward, two steps back, like that bad Paula Abdul song from the early '90s. Which is as true of her career as anybody's.

It rubs us the wrong way, I know, when we feel like we're not making professional headway or good music anymore. Still, you can sometimes only see progress (and cops) in the rearview mirror, and getting to that point can actually involve turning sideways or even going in reverse. But there's no such thing as a wrong direction so long as you're going after learning. Although that answer won't get you out of a ticket.

Because at this point in your career, how far do you really have to fall? To be worrying about making an extra few thousand bucks—although that might finally push you above the poverty line—or becoming a "senior whatever" right now is

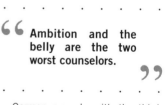

> **Ambition and the belly are the two worst counselors.**

—German proverb, with the third being whoever you get stuck talking to at the college career center

completely losing the plot of the entry level. The point, rather, is to be exploring and discovering and working a whole bunch of shit jobs you can have a laugh about in ten years. Hopefully not from your new shit job.

So if this great opportunity in your lap doesn't come with a sexier title or a better 401(k) match, don't reflexively thumb your nose at it. Instead, take a careful look at the quality of the work and the quality of the people, and figure out how much you stand to learn and grow at this place—including your current company, if that's where the new cube is.

Work Like an Egyptian

"I think people really need to build their career like a pyramid, not like a ladder," says Carol Bartz, chairman of Autodesk, the world's biggest CAD software maker. "I think too often they go for the almighty promotion, and as a result stay in a very narrow field." (Say, like CAD software making.)

Her advice, instead, is to create a broad base of experience, so you have something solid underneath you when you want to move from industry to industry. (Say, like web software making.)

"But to get to that strong base," Bartz cautions, "you may have to take lateral promotions, or maybe even take a step backward in your career." (Say, like answering phones for a software maker.)

And to that point, you should know that at the executive level, many corporations shuffle the deck all the time to expose their top managers to different parts of the business. (As that goes, even MBA internships are increasingly being built to rotate.) Plus not only will a lateral move often compensate with more responsibility and better work—especially if you go from a place with thousands of employees to someplace with maybe a couple hundred—it'll also make your background that much more round. And recruiters, like rappers, love round. You might even have, and like this would be hard, more fun.

Considering you probably started getting good at the fundamentals of your job shortly after developing motor skills as a child, why not extend your life another six to twelve months at this place and see what else they have to show you.

If it sucks as bad, you can still go shopping. And now you can say you've also done this new thing. Not much different than dating, when you think about it.

Good, Now Go Tell *Him* What to Do

"Yet many people who end up in such managerial positions are promoted not for their managerial skills, but for their excellence in other jobs."

—From *The Witch Doctors* (which doesn't specify what "other jobs" we might be talking about)

Finding Your Work - Lie Balance

❝ The world is full of willing people, some willing to work, the rest willing to let them. ❞

—American poet Robert Frost, who was willing to accept the Pulitzer four times for observations like this

Lie no. 58
The Company Cares about Your Outside Life

At least they're not so brash about it any more, most of them. Back during the dot-com boom, when I was up in the Silicon Valley, you'd hear startups throw around nonsense terms like "lifestyle company" or "work hard - play hard," when what they really meant was that the company *is* your lifestyle—with the more accurate descriptor being "work hard - drink hard."

Still, they can't be straight about things and make it onto *Fortune* magazine's "100 Best Companies to Work For" list. That takes jazzy corporate initiatives like flextime programs and telecommuting options and mandated vacations. Which are great, so long as you don't actually touch any of them.

Because the face-time mentality is alive and well in Big Business, with the

No Thanks, I'm Full

According to another recent study by CareerBuilder.com, nearly half of all people surveyed said their workloads were too heavy (and another 25 percent felt their boyfriend or girlfriend was too heavy).

Not to doubt them, but it begs the question of why they were taking an online survey to begin with, if they're so busy.

The real stress cases probably never even made it to the site.

bloodshot eyes and sleeping-in-your-clothes thing being worn around the office like a badge of courage. Never mind it's usually a sham, seeing as most workers buy up their dedication on the black market: Just watch, where employees flick on

their desk lamps, spread out some important-looking papers, maybe drape a jacket over the back of their chair...and then quietly excuse themselves to get the hell out of there.

Newbies are especially vulnerable to the work-imitating-life bit, given where they just came from. College, after all, blurred the line practically clean, what with the typical eighteen-hour day of eating, studying, classes, napping, eating, napping, studying—no, sorry, eating—drinking, drinking, drinking, screwing, vomiting, and, heroically, napping again. Some organizations have even tried to re-create this kind of environment with their tricked-out "corporate campuses," featuring everything from on-site daycare and dry cleaning, to gyms, basketball courts, game rooms, masseuses (no happy endings, though), and all-you-can-gain cafeterias. No cost to you. Unless you count your identity, I suppose.

To be fair, some of these places are pretty fun (if a little cultish), and management does care about their employees' health. But it's not altruism at work; it's capitalism. If they could get you as profitable without having to do all this, they'd have the foosball tables and treadmills back on the truck that day. To them it's all overhead. They just need to keep you within walking distance of the computer until your eyes go buggy.

So enjoy the perks, to be sure; grab all you can. Just don't get the free soda twisted with free love. It's *never* free, my friend.

Lie no. 59
You Have to Work Harder at the Beginning

This also goes back to that just-out-of-prison mentality. When you don't have a hundred pages a night to (not) read, or aren't playing chicken with ink poisoning over those tiny illegible crib notes on your arm, there's an overcompensation thing that often goes on. The M.O. has always been to spend your nights studying—or at least to bitch about studying. Or, at the very least, to feel guilty for not bitching about the studying you should really be bitching about.

But now that your time is actually your own (if you want to count getting home just soon enough to eat, get gas, and go unconscious), grunts sometimes feel like they need to be doing more for the company. It's nothing, certainly, that can't wait until tomorrow. Not unless you can find some urgency I can't in cataloguing those presentations that sat uncatalogued for the three years prior to you getting there.

But newbies, and especially the overachievers, often have a hard time

> ❝ If you're not working on your ideal day, you're working on someone else's. ❞
>
> —Career coach Marjorie Blanchard, who really does both, now doesn't she?

getting unstuck from school mode, and don't really know what to do with themselves otherwise—now that there aren't any on-campus clubs or societies or drunken classmates to hold them up for keg-stands.

But this is dangerous, and not just for the risk of you becoming boring at the handful of parties you get invited to now. No, there's actually a good chunk of psychological research out there showing that the patterns for decision-making you start to form during your twenties and thirties tend to stay with you for the rest of your years. Meaning a no-holds-barred work life today can lead to an alone-in-the-bar love life tomorrow. And for proof, just look at some of the more pathetic cases around the office; they didn't get that way overnight. (And just think if you had to room with them in college.)

The point is that there's a whole world outside to be taken in through the pores, and you need to go do some of that as a grunt. Work will always be there, but your youth won't. So go get laid before you get all wrinkly, huh? You'll thank me.

Free Time Isn't Even Free

In their article, "Must Success Cost So Much?" authors Bartolomé and Evans conclude that when work is overwhelming and unsatisfying (i.e., entry and level), negative emotional spillover will soak a person's private life—"no matter how little he travels, how much time he spends at home, or how frequently he takes a vacation."

Good thing you're not wasting your time on any of those, eh?

—From *Harvard Business Review on Work and Life Balance*

They've done studies, scientists have, to see how much work a person can do in one day. (Certain corporations, some of which I've got on my résumé, do this kind of experiment daily.) And after more than a hundred years of stopwatches and assembly lines and ergonomic chairs, they still can't say for sure. Especially when it's in the computer-screen glare of "mental work," because how do you measure that anyway? How strong your headache gets? Maybe how big your hemorrhoids grow? No, it must be cholesterol level, because at least then you could do statistics—and nobody believes anything without statistics. Except for statisticians, who know better.

Regardless, it's not a one-to-one correlation, work and success; the closer relationship, in fact, is between long hours and being single. (Success is most strongly tied to having an uncle in management somewhere, or enjoying a high tolerance for drugs and the ability to play an electric guitar really

> 66 **By working faithfully eight hours a day, you may get to be a boss and work twelve hours a day.** 99
>
> —Robert Frost (again), who sure knew a lot about business life for being a poet

loudly.) So don't think that pulling all-nighters in the cube is going to get you anywhere. Besides plotted against by your slack-ass coworkers, who you're making look bad.

Once in a great while, you'll see the sun come up through the sealed windows of your office building (which aren't sealed only to keep the cool air from jumping out, by the way). But that's only when your group has really made a train wreck of a project, and you're about to blow the second or third

deadline extension. Otherwise there's just no reason. Plus think back to how productive you *really* were when you were trying to memorize calculus equations at four in the morning. With Starbucks being closed.

Which is also backed up by science. Cutting your siestas short has been shown to lead to lower overall work quality, greater numbers of errors and oversights, impaired memory, and, we can't forget, irritability. Now, you get plenty of that already without the help of an always-made bed. Rather, the smartest move here is to do like you usually did during your late-afternoon anthropology lecture. (You know, sitting right where the sun leaks in, with the calming white noise of whatever the professor is going on about. Best naps ever.)

Not sleeping enough has even been linked to depression—where rising in the wee hours suggests your normal rhythms are off. Or that you have your alarm set too damn early. Either way it's not smart, so stop it and go get some extra zzz's. Didn't college teach you anything?

> " The amount of sleep required by the average person is about five minutes more. "
>
> —American humorist Max Kauffman, who might've noted it was at least an hour for any 8 a.m. class

Lie no. 61
Burnout Only Happens to Older Workers

Did you know we've now passed Japan as the workaholic capital of the world? Granted, they had a lot more drunken karaoke than us to distract them along the way, but it still wasn't easy.

And it wasn't all orchestrated by those I-left-reality-in-my-other-pants managers running around the office, making sure everybody else has high blood pressure, too. We're talking all levels of the workforce, with grunts like you being just as likely to overcommit: day, night, home, abroad, in a box, with a fox. And the typical markings of any corporate routine—coming in on the weekends, flipping open the laptop at home, nixing vacations, working through colds, the flu, Ebola, SARS—are also the typical markings of eventual burnout.

When there's nothing to define the boundary between

All Pooped Out

Forty-two percent of American laborers feel spent by the time they get home, according to data cited by business thinker Charles Handy.

We're all caught, he says, in the cycle of working to get tired, to go to sleep, to wake up and get tired again.

Sounds pretty sad when you put it like that. Same thing goes for eating and lovemaking, after all, but nobody's complaining there…

—From *The Hungry Spirit*

—English statesman Lord Chesterfield
(except newbies usually don't do
either)

work and everything else (assuming there's anything to even keep apart), the stresses of the day never go away. This, in turn, builds over time, leading to things like chronic fatigue, cynicism, emotional swings, and even being more self-critical. Once again, you don't need any help with that; your boss has more than got it covered.

People who really love what they do, by contrast (yes, we've been able to find a few), report feelings of excitement and release from the hustle—even resulting in more rewarding interpersonal relationships and healthier weight and sleep patterns. They also seem to do less dying from things like strokes, heart attacks, and strangulation with their own necktie or pashmina.

Which is telling you, in sum, to slow down until you get there. Unless you're that turned on by filing, I don't know.

Beach Reading?

A 2004 survey by the Families and Work Institute found that 42 percent of Americans do some form of work while on vacation. And only 14 percent of us are taking the standard two weeks to begin with.

On top of that, the average person needs about three days to begin to relax. So if they're squeezing in a week's break, it's actually less than four days. Not counting packing, airport time, and the gripping depression that sets in a day or two before returning.

Enjoy your half-day off!

Lifestyles of the Rich and Sedated

Speaking of the blues, here's an interesting little scenario: There are upwards of 3,500,000 households in the U.S. boasting a net worth of or above a million bucks, with more earners under the age of fifty than above it. That's a first in this country.

Another first is the number of individuals who've been diagnosed with depression, as the National Institute for Health Care Management Foundation (hell of an acronym there) clocks antidepressants as the most commonly purchased prescription drug among Americans—above ulcer, asthma, and even cholesterol pills. And you know how fat we're all getting.

Could it be that our drug-happy doctors are overdoing it? Sending their patients to the pharmacy helps pay the lease on their Jaguars, so that's part of it. But a recent study by WebMD also found that financial issues help to bring on the rainy days in workers' heads, and that businesses are footing an estimated $43 billion a year in absenteeism, reduced productivity, and medical bills as a result.

How does it all tie together? You can do your own math, but it seems to me that we're getting pretty worn out chasing after the almighty dollar. Not much point in being rich if you need to be medicated to actually enjoy it, no?

Most guys have their priorities dictated to them by their penis and their wallet (which you can really see come together nicely in a gentlemen's club). Women aren't that far back, either, with their top two being finding a husband and finding a shoe sale. And to be able to earn any of that, you've usually got to earn a pretty decent living first.

So it's not uncommon to watch grunts fresh out of school—where everyone was poor and condoms were free—now line up along the fast track, racing against professionals who've been cashing company checks for years. (And most of whom have managed to dig themselves further into debt than even you by keeping up appearances.) Problem is you'll never be able to keep up like that—and just a minute ago you said you didn't even want to—plus

Balanced Sheet?

So PricewaterhouseCoopers came to campus for something other than to snag smart accounting majors: Turns out they also conducted a survey of twenty-five hundred students to see what they wanted in a first job.

Even more surprising was the result, with 57 percent naming "attaining a balance between personal life and career" as their primary professional goal.

Freedom more important than money? To poor kids? Smells like another scandal to me…

there's no finish line to cross anyway.

That lesson typically only comes with time and an ulcer and a few failed relationships, though—meaning newbies often find themselves seventy, eighty hours a week into it before they realize what's going on. So let me stop you before you really get started: If you're gunning for the promotion that's going to cost you your friendships and youthful-looking skin and the ability to talk about anything but work or the 1 a.m. *SportsCenter* rerun, you need to ask yourself if that's a promotion you really want.

We'll get much deeper later on in the book, but it's not like people don't get it—that they can't see what's going on. Back them into a corner, and they'll admit it's their fault that the closest relationship they have is with their cat or their vibrator. So at least be honest with yourself, and make it a conscious decision to have your Saturday nights be about Häagen-Dazs and *Sex and the City* DVDs and phone calls to mom.

> **It's a shame the only thing a man can do for eight hours is work. He can't eat for eight hours; he can't drink for eight hours; he can't make love for eight hours.**

—Nobel Prize novelist William Faulkner, who I think would be contradicted by Sting on that last one

I'm not saying you blow off your responsibilities at the office either, obviously, but that you figure out what belongs to you and what belongs to the company. Like not labeling your food in the fridge, if you don't eat it, someone else in the house will.

The no-time-to-[blank] excuse is, nine times out of ten, total bullshit. People find a way to do things all the time that, if you or I looked at their calendar, *we'd* go fire their assistant for booking them like that.

Say you were to sit down and really look at how, exactly, you spend your days and nights—which would be emotional, so do it in private. There's no doubt you'd find two, three hours, minimum, that you basically piss away doing nothing. And not that all this nothing-time needs to, or even should, go away; a little procrastination and bad TV is good for you. But don't turn around, then, and say work is stopping you from doing what you really want to. How often did you let that happen, after all, with school and parents?

It's a question of priorities, like we just talked about. And there's no magic to it: You decide to go do something, and then you go do it. Pretty straightforward. Now, certain project

> 66 I always arrive late at the office, but I make up for it by leaving early. 99

—Charles Lamb, who reminds me of a guy we used to call "Mr. LIFO" (Last In, First Out; it's an accounting term. Anyway, really funny if you're there.)

deadlines and pissy managers are going to slow you down once in a while, sure; but those should be the exception. And if they're not, you need to go have one of those heart-to-hearts with yourself, and make sure this is really how you want to live. Or at least see if you'd get caught for beating your boss to death with his own shoe.

Research on "balanced people"—don't ask me how they're screened—shows that they tend to build rituals and practices and targets into their everyday routines, which help them do all the stuff the rest of us would get strung-out on caffeine and amphetamines trying to squeeze in. And by sticking to these plans (almost) no matter what, they also gain a sense of control in their lives, and can tell day-in and day-out how big of a sellout they're being.

So the entry level is the place to start getting good at your "me time." It only gets busier, I promise, as the title (and your belly) starts to get bigger...

Here Comes the Sun

"Your company measures its priorities. People also need to place metrics around their priorities," advises Vinod Khosla, founding CEO of Sun Microsystems (who I'm sure has databases running to track when his kids brush their teeth).

Most recently a partner at Kleiner Perkins Caufield & Byers, one of Silicon Valley's premiere venture capital firms—which, incidentally, funded the startup I was with—Khosla works about fifty hours a week when he could easily put in one hundred. But to Vinod, it's more important that he's home for dinner with the fam exactly twenty-five nights a month (not sure if there's an adjustment in February).

"Having a target number is key," Khosla explains. "I know people in my business who are lucky if they make it home five nights a month. I don't think that I'm any less productive than those people."

He's certainly no less rich, with a net worth recently around a **billion** dollars.

Lie no. 64
You Can't Say No

A nyone who's spent any length of time in a bar or MBA admissions office knows that people say no all the time. (Some more nicely than others, *Harvard*.) You've just got to be a little more delicate about it with entry level bosses—whose egos are sadly puffed in knowing some punk college grad can't reject them.

Which is why managers love to dress up "nice-to-haves" as "must-haves," when all they really want is to casually admire the thing sitting on their desk for a while. So before you go skipping out on Texas hold'em night or passing up *Bridget Jones's Diary* with the girls—it gets better after the seventh or eighth time, I hear—try to tease out what kind of rush this particular assignment is really in.

Your boss's memory, as we already know, is about as good as your old stoner friends from school. So maybe give it a little jog here by running down the list of all of the other high-priority work he has you

> **Learn to say 'No!' It will be of more use to you than to be able to read Latin.**

—Nineteenth-century preacher Charles Spurgeon, back when this was a compelling argument

scrambling to get done for him. Heard all at once, he'll see just how irrational he's being, and promptly pass the job off to one of your other teammates. That, or offer to buy you takeout at your desk tonight, depending.

Things, admittedly, do get a little more gray when it's a senior or interdepartmental bigwig who's coming to you with palms upturned. They probably don't ask that often. And when they do, it's usually with the implied promise of some kind of payback down the line. Which, tough for you, probably also includes the other sort if you turn them down.

These have to be a judgment call, a case-by-case thing. Some people you know are going to make good on their promises, and some are just looking for a new head to take a dump on. So feel the situation out—how important the project is (or, for that matter, how important *they* are) versus your existing workload and whatever else you've got going on in your private life—and then call the ball. Some you'll get into a nice back-scratching arrangement with, and some you'll give the finger and a big grin.

Waving the Red Flag

"I never want to say no, especially to our sponsors," reveals NASCAR champ and pretty-boy Jeff Gordon.

"But if I didn't learn to say no, I wasn't going to be able to do my job. And my job is what got me the sponsors in the first place." (Again, looking good on a cereal box also didn't hurt.)

All I need now is for Jeff to explain why these companies pay so much to have their logos blur together on an object taking repeated left turns at 200 mph.

> **For fast-acting relief, try slowing down.**

—Actress and comedienne Lily Tomlin, who herself hasn't slowed down since the early '70s

Even if they are going to hook you up, though, that shouldn't come at the expense of you hooking up outside the office, as we'll talk about next. So you not only have to consider what you've already got scheduled, but also what you'd like to schedule. Love and happiness, after all, don't come by chilling in the office, no matter how much you like your job. That takes someone you can *leave* the office for. And make out with.

Back in 2000, a virus called the "Luv Bug" infected millions of computers. Why'd so many people catch it? Because the programmers wrote "I love you" in the subject line.

Shows you how desperate we all are for a little affection. And it's not like love is going to just land in your inbox one day (I'll come back to online dating in a minute). Left neglected, in fact, and none of that sexy underwear you've been waiting to use is going to fit by the time you really need it.

Which goes against everything we all thought a good job and a nice car would land us with. Not that we have either of those yet, but that's beside the point. Even then, we'd probably have to smash up our Mercedes to finally exchange numbers with someone who's interested in us.

> " Ann Landers said that you are addicted to sex if you have it more than three times a day, and that you should seek professional help. I have news for Ann Landers: The only way I'm going to get sex three times a day is if I seek professional help. "
>
> —*Tonight Show* host Jay Leno, who'd probably rather have sex with one of his cars

But between the working lunches, the working dinners, the working travel, and the general working-back of your sense of humor and hairline, at what point are you supposed to start working toward a relationship? No clean answer to this one either, other than to say you've just got to make it a priority.

The number of singles in this country has gone up by more than 20 percent since the 1970s—and it's not like people were getting any more sleep or money or r-e-s-p-e-c-t back when they were on acid. Rather, there was just more of an emphasis on having some style and a personal life to show it off in. Even if that style did come in a powder blue leisure suit.

Not that we're going back to the 9-to-5 in place when IBM was just starting to recruit ex-hippies (thank God). Yet there's still room to push back on your assignments once in a while, and make sure disco isn't dead forever. Besides, you're only a recession and a layoff away from missing all the meetings you want to, so let's keep it in perspective, shall we?

After all, the right man or woman will go out with you no matter how poor and raggedy you are. And that's a definition of success we can all come away feeling good about.

Two of a Kind

"Having sex is like playing bridge: If you don't have a good partner, you'd better have a good hand."

—Woody Allen

Lie no. 66
You'll Find "The One" in a Bar

Seeing as most of our jobs drive us to drink, or at least our friends do, grunts typically end up trying to meet women in bars. Occasionally for more than just that night. Except only the women know what they're doing.

Because every night, girls, is ladies night at the pub, and drinks are on him if you play it right: You may have a boyfriend, after all, in which case he's wasting his cash. You may have only recently gotten out of a relationship and aren't looking to meet anyone, in which case he's wasting his cash. You may be excited about a new guy and don't want to shop around anymore, in which case he's wasting his cash. You may be on a girls' night out, in which case not only is he wasting his cash, but you're having an even better time taking it from him because you can laugh about it with all of your friends.

And if she's really hot, gentlemen, this is happening every time she goes out. Usually by guys much

> 66 Instead of getting married again, I'm going to find a woman I don't like and just give her a house. 99
>
> —Rocker Rod Stewart, after divorcing supermodel Rachel Hunter

less qualified than you. Which also means she's got a ton of practice at helping you waste your cash.

Much smarter to invest your money into your own inebriation. Or, smarter still, into trying to get invited to private parties and events. There's no better way, in fact, to meet a girl—and, ladies, this is equally true of men—than at a shindig organized by a friend, coworker, contact, whomever. Especially by a *female* friend, coworker, or contact, because they have *other* female friends, coworkers, and contacts to introduce you to.

First off, gentlemen, you've already got a vouch just by being there, which makes you easy to meet (and gives her an easy out, should you turn out to be an idiot or a freak). Second, and more importantly, you've already met most, if not all, of the chicks your buddies know. And chances are they've hooked up with them at some point, which is never the right mental image to go into it with.

Deeper Thoughts

"Whenever someone asks me to define love, I usually think for a minute, then I spin around and pin the guy's arm behind his back. *Now* who's asking the questions?"

—Jack Handey

Now, guys and girls alike, once your roster of acquaintances is tapped, and the agenda of house-warmings and dinner parties dries up, you can always start to look into groups to join and classes to take. Say, like Lamaze or CODA or something from *Fight Club*.

It goes back to ducking out of the office a little early, of course, but things like professional associations, young alumni groups, continuing education workshops, community college classes, outdoors clubs, coed sports teams, churches/temples/the occult—all are great places to meet like-minded others. Who, incidentally, you already know are receptive to meeting *other* like-minded others (or at least are aware they're in danger of it). Plus even if you don't land a mate, you've at least got something enjoyable to do with your nights and weekends that doesn't involve video games or Kleenex or your self-esteem.

> 66 Sex is a momentary itch; love never lets you go. 99
>
> —Not sure who said this, but I like it (although it does remind me of VD).

If push really does come to shove, there's speed dating and online personals to resort to. I'll put in my $0.02 about the Internet thing next, but generally speaking, anything's better than a bar or a club if you're really looking for love. Although if you just want to go gyrate against a stranger or get fondled at random, I know a couple of great spots if you're ever out here in LA.

Lie no. 67
Online Dating Is the Answer

Internet dating, mostly shedding its creepy and taboo origins in the earliest chat rooms on AOL, has grown into a $300 million-plus industry—largely built up by all the cube-dwellers like you stuck behind their desk ten or twelve hours a day. Which I guess makes it kind of like eBay, but for people.

And despite all of the clever niches being carved out—like Jewish, Indian, and gay-only sites—as well as the more than fifteen million subscribers to reigning heavyweight Match.com, the whole space is still pretty sketchy. Like any kind of classified ad out there, you've got to assume that you're not getting the whole story: The seller almost always knows something the buyer doesn't, and that the buyer doesn't find out until after they've lost their money, or gotten naked, or opened up a particular drawer when somebody wasn't home.

All Logged On, Baby!

It's a buyer's market if you're a woman and looking for love online: An estimated 60 percent of dating-site visitors are male (or at least claim to be).

Although, according to web research authority Neilsen//NetRatings, about 10 percent of Internet matchmaking users aren't exactly single either.

Plus another 1 or 2 percent, I'm sure, who would be jailed if anyone found what was on their hard drives.

I'm a little unclear as to how the mind doesn't rebel at some point when you know you're going to meet this person, and watch all of the lies you've strung together start to unravel. Yet you still regularly see outrageous claims of being "petite" or "smart" or "female." Which really fleshes out the highpoints of the typical profile, such as "I enjoy trying new restaurants" and "love to have fun!" You too? Christ, this must be destiny!

At the end of the day, this is still a blind date. And since chemistry can only happen—or not—in person, skip the marathon calls, keep the witty notes to a minimum, forget anyone more than fifty miles away, and don't plan anything over an hour. Oh, and wear comfortable shoes, a pair you can run in.

Remember, the Web is great for getting things like news and books—not so much for getting things like husbands and wives. Although I'm not saying you can't; just be sure you keep a sense of humor and your patience. Plus maybe some pepper spray.

Online Dating Calculator

Better do the math before you meet your mate! Here's how to find the real numbers for your online lover:

Height

Subtract 3" from any man's listing, minimum.

Weight

Don't trust the photo; this is when she was on speaking terms with her metabolism. Add 15 lbs., at least. (25 lbs. if she leaves the "Physical Activities" field empty.)

Age

If she looks 25, she's 40; if she looks 20, she's 13.

Salary

- Under $25,000: Stupidly honest; probably a nice guy
- $25,000–$50,000: Scraping by on $20,000, at best
- $50,000–$75,000: Boring, but has a secure job
- $75,000–$100,000: He doesn't have time for you
- Over $100,000: Liar or rich parents (just your type!)

Johm Lennon is over-quoted as saying that life is what happens while you're busy making other plans. Not that he's wrong, but at the entry level, it's usually what happens while you're busy making other copies.

Which, I'm convinced, is a major step back from pre-industrial days, when people worked much more like college students: Waking up late; taking long lunches and midday naps; banging out all-night working sessions; banging out all-night drinking sessions. Now we've got cubes and timesheets and, ugh, khakis.

Not that you can do much about it, other than cutting-out every now and again. Yes, I'm absolutely advocating taking time off when it's not on the schedule: Whole days, half days, not coming back from meetings, shutting off your cell. Guilt-free.

You can't get out of hand with it, obviously, but hell—if the sun's out and you can't deal with being inside, then

Always the Real Thing

"Imagine life as a game in which you are juggling five balls: work, family, health, friends, and spirit.

"Work is a rubber ball. If you drop it, it will bounce back. But the other four balls are made of glass. If you drop one of these, they will never be the same."

—Brian Dyson, former CEO, Coca-Cola Enterprises

don't be. I guarantee you'll forget that day if you spend it working. But you might just make a happy little memory for yourself with whatever else you decide to do. Especially if that whatever has a nice smile and a swimsuit.

When you go too fast, there's never an opportunity to be peaceful and reflective and to try to make sense of everything. And not that you have to sit around "ohm-ing"

in lotus position either, but you're really going to miss out on a lot of life if you don't miss a little work in between.

Which won't stop you from getting a raise or getting promoted, provided you're not stupid about it (e.g., flaking on clients, missing deadlines, crank calling your boss). This is just your time to take a breath, take care of some personal things, take the dog for a walk, take your friend out lunch, take a trip to someplace you've always wanted to go. Even to your couch at one in the afternoon to watch soaps, if that's your thing.

Recreation, in its time and place, is as proper as anything else you do. (Much more so than your silly job, usually.) So give yourself the distance from the office every so often to goof-off and recharge the battery and make sure you don't live one of those unconsidered lives.

In other words, if you're going to be an asshole workaholic, at least do it on purpose.

> 66 I tell you, we are here on Earth to fart around, and don't let anybody tell you any different. 99
>
> —Kurt Vonnegut, and that's that

9

Do What You Love, and You'll Probably Starve

· · · · · · · · ·

66 **I've got all the money I'll ever need, if I die by four o'clock.** 99

· · · · · · · · ·

—Old-time comedian Henny Youngman,
which most grunts can't even say

Lie no. 69
Most Careers Are Carefully Chosen

People usually just sort of fall into what they do for a living—with money usually jutting the foot out that trips them.

They know somebody who knows somebody who slept with somebody, the story goes, and hey, we've got a real cushy job over here if you want it. And hey, why not, right? It's just that five, seven years later—not even looking where they're going—they've somehow gotten themselves very entrenched in an industry that they never liked very much to begin with.

Which is why they make snooze buttons so big on alarm clocks. Waking up, in fact, is the worst part of the day for I don't know how many Americans: Confronted with some drop-out radio talk show host, and the realization that they've got to go do this awful, awful thing again. Plus have to sit in traffic to go do it.

And those scientists from before, who were throwing all that math around about employee productivity—yeah, they

> 66 **When a fellow says it ain't the money but the principle of the thing, it's the money.** 99
>
> —Artemus Ward, one of America's first stand-up comics (and, it sounds like, business thinkers)

were at it again. Except this time they came back with a number: 60 percent. But now this figure represents how much of your life you can expect to render unto Caesar: working, sitting at

work (two separate things, clearly), getting ready for work, commuting to work, thinking about work, thinking about whacking your manager with a stick. And that's on top of the other third of our lives we spend in bed—for better or worse reasons—leaving about a month and a half total before you die to go do everything else you've ever wanted to do with your life. After grocery shopping.

Making it a good idea to be a little more choosy about what kind of cube you want to bang your head against every morning. And it's not like moving into a bigger one is necessarily going to make it hurt any less: Results from a mess of interviews with a mess of people who went back to business school—trying to jumpstart their careers in finance or technology or whatever else they talk about on CNBC—show that they aren't any happier or more fulfilled with an MBA than they were without it. (Although they *are* in debt to their eyeballs, so it's a tradeoff, like anything else.)

When asked, also, who they'd most like to have lunch with, the bulk of these Wall Street wannabes said they'd

> **A good rule of thumb is if you've made it to thirty-five and your job still requires you to wear a name-tag, you've made a serious vocational error.**

—Comedian Dennis Miller, whose show was cancelled by HBO because he's too smart for everyone

rather break bread with a humanitarian or social leader than the CEO of their choice. Which is also true, incidentally, when asked of most CEOs.

So, whatever kind of job you want to cut your teeth on as a grunt, make sure you really do want it. Or at least know what you want to get out of it before you get out. Otherwise you might just wake up one day in your mid-forties, as a mid-level manager, at a place that still has mid-1960s office furniture, and have yourself a little midlife crisis. And that's just way too much mediocrity. If you're going to crash, at least do it with some style.

There's this license plate rim I remember seeing some years back with that old comic strip character Ziggy, offering the caution to other drivers: "Don't follow me, I'm lost too!" And putting aside the kind of person who would actually stick such a thing on their car, there's something to be said for the honesty.

Now if only we were that candid about our careers, if not so tacky. Here, though, it's really just the opposite, with people either thinking they know what they're doing and being wrong, or subconsciously realizing they don't and scrambling to hide that fact—from themselves as much as anybody else. Which makes them a lot like another kind of character…*lemmings.*

You know, those little purple and green buggers from the video game—all plodding forward and falling off cliffs and going splat. They seem to think the guy in front of them knows where he's headed, and so they just sort of line up and mindlessly trod

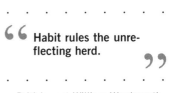

66 **Habit rules the unre-flecting herd.** 99

—British poet William Wordsworth, who made a habit of knocking-up French girls along. (Who got the brilliant idea to market a game of tiny suicidal animals to children, I still haven't figured out.)

There's an old maxim that says if everyone's headed in the same direction, it's probably wrong. Which is also probably why fewer than 5 percent of twentysomethings report having found their calling—even (or should I say especially) after tacking an MBA onto their résumé. Instead of looking within, they're all too busy looking around: Worrying about what everyone else is doing, and wringing their hands over the suspicion that these other guys know something they don't.

So I'm going to let you in on a little secret...everybody's full of shit. Okay, maybe that's not such a secret. Particularly in Corporate America. But it can be a hard one to separate yourself from when trying to make heads or tails of your career. Believe me, they don't have it figured out any more than you do—even if they look like they've totally got it together. That's just marketing.

You ask people in their thirties and forties about having found their calling, and they're just as likely to look at you cross-eyed as anybody your age you meet in a bar. Most of them checked out a long time ago, conceding that this is what they've ended up doing—like it or not—and so they might as well get on board and make the best of it. Same thing for the relationships a lot of them are in, too, which is even sadder: "It's not that I don't love you, honey; it's just that I probably can't do any better, and I'm settling on you. So what's for dinner?"

> " Only those who risk going too far can possibly find out how far one can go. "
>
> —T. S. Eliot, describing the mindset I approached my early career with

If you're waiting to take your cue from the pack, then, just keep in mind where most lemmings end up. And this game doesn't have a reset button.

Henry David Thoreau, in *Walden,* talks of most men living lives of "quiet desperation." True enough. But at least this quiet desperation has indoor plumbing, you could argue, which is the price you pay for not having to wipe yourself with a leaf.

But what about people mentioning they'd rather spend time talking with Gandhi than Bill Gates? If that's the case, then why aren't they out doing non-profit or social work instead of playing computer monkey and buying $400 Prada shoes? And not that these life-affirming gigs are so easy to come by—or that they necessarily pay a living wage even if you do—but that's not the point. The point is that people don't even hear what they're saying. Much less believe it.

Because if folks really listened, they'd recognize the contradiction between what they're doing with their lives, and what they actually think is important to do with their lives. And, again, not everyone is suited to save the whales;

66 **We work to become, not to acquire.** 99

—U.S. author Elbert Hubbard, who ended up acquiring a lot of water on the sinking ship *Lusitania*

left up to most people, in fact, Flipper would've choked on one of those six-pack plastic holder thingies a long time ago. But there is something, chances are, that they're just as passionate about—music, teaching, writing, design, stripping—and they're not pursuing it because it's too risky or too hard or would cut too far into their Barneys account. Which they can't even pay to begin with, but did you see how that sweater fit?

Going back to our favorite literary hippie, what Thoreau was really talking about was *values:* Doing something with your life that you actually enjoy, gain fulfillment from, feel a sense of purpose with. Which isn't just some romantic, pie-in-the-sky

> " I do not try to dance better than anyone else. I only try to dance better than myself. "
>
> —Russian ballet dancer Mikhail Baryshnikov, who also tried to act better than himself as Carrie's love interest on *Sex and the City*

idea—even if the example I'm using sort of is. And even if the corporate entry level isn't exactly the place where you're very likely to "find yourself." Unless you mean finding yourself as in, "How in the hell did I ever end up *here*?"

Some of this is unavoidable (e.g., that hard-reality-of-life kind of thing Dad's so hung up on), and a lot of it has to do with learning about what you want your job to mean to you—what you want to get out of it, besides the cash for the 21 percent interest on that Barneys bill.

When you get past the dues-paying part, though, and are finally over all the superficial stuff—the timing of which is different for everyone—just make sure you're putting as much energy into accounting for the stuff you're made of as you put into accounting for the stuff you make. Twice as much if you're actually an accountant.

Because there's no one career that's intrinsically better than the other—no matter what it does or doesn't pay. It's only about what's better to you: what gets you lost in the flow, what makes you feel like the truest version of yourself, what you really knock people out by doing. In short, whatever it is, just make sure you love it. (And that you stay out of Barneys.)

Lie no. 72
Jobs Are Often Fulfilling and Enjoyable

More Americans say "goodbye, cruel world" on Monday mornings than on any other day or at any other time. That's also the favorite time for men to have 75 percent of their sudden heart attacks.

I was only making an analogy with the hara-kiri lemmings; I wasn't trying to be morbid or anything. But I guess there's really something about starting a work-week that people don't cope with very well. Whether they tell their bodies it's enough already, or vice-versa.

I haven't been able to get any sales figures for how bars do on Monday evenings, but I bet you those are pretty high, too (and not just during football season). Because where else can you get sloppy and really have it out with yourself? It's the perfect spot, really, to sit down with a trusted coworker, and explain

But, My Stapler...

Nosy CareerBuilder.com did another survey in 2004, and found that one in four workers is currently dissatisfied with their job—a 20 percent increase over 2001.

Another 60 percent, on top of that, plan to give their current boss the finger within the next two years, and move on to something they're betting they'll dislike less.

Personally, I thought these numbers would've been higher. Maybe they meant that one in four workers is dissatisfied enough to set fire to the building, and the rest would just loot the place?

Working Wounded

"It is, above all (or beneath all), about daily humiliations," as Studs Terkel so grimly puts it about jobs in his 1972 classic book, *Working* (a 762-page monster I didn't get around to reading until about four years after it was assigned to me in college). "To survive the day is triumph enough for the walking wounded among the great many of us."

What's sad is that not much has changed in the past thirty-plus years. Most people still do that "Monday through Friday sort of dying" he laments, and feel stuck doing it.

If you've got to be humiliated—which you don't—it might as well be in trying something you really want. Professionally or in the bedroom.

how one of two people are going to die, and here's what's in it for them—besides a new boss—if they want to help.

Now I really am being morbid, but still not that far from the reality of things. It's staggering how many people genuinely detest what they do for a living, and even more staggering how many of them simply put up with it. Oh, they'll hop from job to job every few years, but just to make more money doing the same thing they hate. Which is even more crazy from a college-only perspective, where you dropped a class in twenty minutes flat after deciding the professor was a blowhard, and that having the final on the last Friday of the semester wasn't going to work for you.

This isn't fate, I promise, but you're going to find plenty of solidarity if you want to go commiserate about work. More importantly, though, you can't get discouraged by all of these victims of their careers: Nobody's doing this to them but themselves, and you should see it as a sad and cautionary tale about what can happen if you're not careful. Sort of a driver's-ed *Red Asphalt* film, but for jobs.

The only place you have to go, instead, is up, and with fair warning about what you might be in for some days. Even the best careers have their downswings. Just make sure yours aren't *all* the way down, huh?

> " Oh, you hate your job? Why didn't you say so? There's a support group for that. It's called EVERYBODY, and they meet at the bar. "
>
> —Comedian Drew Carey, who does know his audience, I'll give him that

Lie no. 73
Work Is about Money, Not Purpose

Your father's and grandfather's generation would fight you on this one, and hard. From where they came from (probably Europe for Grandpa and suburbia for Dad), it was about responsibility to the family. Work wasn't something you loved; it was something you *endured,* and proudly. No wonder they always had a drink when they came home.

Which is also partly why Gen X and Y have such a bad rep today. The idea of wanting to fancy your job—to people who crossed the Atlantic without a shower—somehow feels wrong and self-indulgent. Never mind that you've spent the better part of the last two decades enduring your own tiresome journey, through the liberal

---

You're Good Enough, You're Smart Enough, and Gosh Darn It, People Like You!

Artists, as a rule, make a living selling their art. (And working in restaurants.) Don't tell that to American painter John Singer Sargent, though, who brushed a panel of roses to his canvas that was so good, he refused to part with it.

Turning down offers that would've equaled a year's worth of tips, easy, Sargent simply wouldn't sell. Nobody understood.

What they didn't know was that whenever Sargent was feeling insecure about his abilities, he would look at this work and be reminded he did something great. Expensive confidence booster, sure; but how many of us have "our painting"?

arts. Different kind of trip, sure; but you definitely still needed that drink at night.

Whatever, there's no point in being poor and educated in this country if you can't have some fun paying back your school loans. We'll get into how to deal with your parents later

on, but know for now that you can't let anyone strong-arm you into doing what you do for the sake of "security" or "practicality" or "rent." You've got a lot of working years ahead of you—whatever you decide to do—and if you don't find some value in your career, that's a pretty empty way to spend nearly two-thirds of your life. No matter what you're spending on shoes.

Not that the folks were completely wrong, either—which, annoyingly, they seldom are; you can't completely factor money out of the equation. But so long as you can otherwise manage to pay your bills and eat, sacrificing your passion for a paycheck will be the most expensive thing you ever do.

Pick Up Your Toys!

Philosophers, who have nothing better to think about, have speculated that if we lived in a utopia where everything had already been built, invented, and discovered, scientists and architects would keep on building, inventing, and discovering—but as a *game*.

Provoking thought. Still, it shows that when you really love the work you do, it stops being work, and starts being *play*. Complicated and intense play, granted, but play nonetheless. Like the kind philosophers do.

Kids, too. It's only about fun with them, never the outcome. I mean, how many long-labored Lego structures are left standing when it's dinnertime? Not the first place youngsters have gotten it right where we haven't...

Lie no. 74
Do What You Love, and You'll Probably Starve

This was the title of an article on MSN written by Martin Nemko, a fairly well-known career counselor who I got into an exchange with.

Mainly over his focus on all the people who've followed their passion, and still haven't earned enough money to pay back their creditors—much less eek out a middle-class living. To which Nemko's solution is taking a safe, predictable, mundane job. "Unless you're a true superstar (brilliant, driven, great personality, or have great connections)," Marty hedges, "give it up." Maybe he should take some of his own advice.

Although what's most goading about it is that there's some truth to what he's saying. Not the sleep-your-life-away part, obviously, but

Love It or Leave It

"If you're not passionate, maybe self-discipline or whatever set of emotions you have, including guilt, might help you work hard," believes former nonprofit director of Outward Bound, Allen Grossman.

But that's not how it's supposed to go. To Allen's way of thinking, you can't even have achievement without love for what's being achieved.

"[Passion] is the wonderful ingredient that brings happiness with success," he concludes. Because of the two, only happiness works on its own.

—From *How They Achieved*

about being poor. If you don't take a "proper" corporate job out of college—and even sometimes if you do—chances are it's going to be mac-'n'-cheese for dinner, and prioritizing which utility you can stand to lose this week. (Hint: Pay your electricity bill before the phone; that's what you have a work number for.) Which is even tougher when you've got friends dropping $200 on sushi and drinks every weekend, being all posh and irritating.

But, hey, that's what love costs. And you got pretty good at being destitute in college, so it's not like you're making some major lifestyle downgrade here. Besides, you've got a great shot at being more than financially comfortable down the line if you're doing something right now that you'd really be doing for free. Well, low to mid-twenties, anyway.

Passionate people are contagious, which is why you see so many of them do so well: They not only blow away everyone they're competing against, but they also get the right kind of people excited (i.e., the kind who can hire/promote them). Again, Nemko's not completely off-base; nobody's saying you're necessarily going to get rich doing something you love. But you won't go hungry, either, if you're smart and honest about it, and don't stop until you get what you want.

Do what you hate, on the other hand, and all that's going to starve is your soul...

> " Money will buy you a pretty good dog, but it won't buy the wag of his tail. "
>
> —Henry Wheeler Shaw, who was really more of a cat person

Don't misunderstand; I'm not saying you go after your dream all balls-to-the-wall, caution-to-the-wind, devil-may-care, pick-your-hyphenate. Not unless you're still getting an allowance.

Otherwise, there are a few things going on here—most important of which is realizing that you can't always turn your passion into a career right away. It takes some patience and honesty, instead—asking yourself the difficult questions, and separating your passion from the cold truth of what's involved. Which is almost always more than you think.

So if starting out in the mailroom is the answer, and there's no way around it, then you'd better get to practicing smiling while being yelled at. But if we're talking about acting, writing, public service, or even starting a business, that's something you can usually do on a volunteer or freelance basis—keeping it to nights and weekends at the beginning. Starting off small

> ❝ The only difference between a caprice and a lifelong passion is that the caprice lasts a little longer. ❞
>
> —Oscar Wilde, who was probably having a tough writing day and feeling all testy when he said this

and slowly connecting with the right people, in fact, is sometimes the most effective way to get to the Big Dream. Although you should still practice smiling while being yelled at, regardless.

And what's to say the shape and color of that dream won't change? More often than not it does, and especially before thirty. Because at that point, you usually haven't done enough working (or enough living) to really have a sense of what's out there, and what you can wake up and still be excited about doing for the next ten, fifteen, twenty years. Plus a lot of people don't find their passion until they have some big "ah ha" life-changing experience. Not that you can or should sit around waiting for one of these, either, but you at least need to be out there exposing yourself to all the different areas of life that catch your eye. Especially if they're single.

> ### Just Mapquest It
>
> "If we knew we were on the right road, having to leave it would mean endless despair. But we are on a road that only leads to a second one and then to a third one and so forth."
>
> —Franz Kafka

Which is true even if your epiphany doesn't happen until you're in your fifties: Plenty of these "unconventional students" you saw looking lost around campus aren't doing it because they got laid off, but because they've already had successful careers doing something else, and want to go try a new field now. Passion, you see, is rarely confined to just one thing, and

> ❝ **To venture causes anxiety. Not to venture is to lose oneself.** ❞
>
> —Sören Kierkegaard, Danish philosopher who thought about damn near everything

your career might very well keep you guessing long into your Viagra years.

The point of all this is to say that life is never that simple or cooperative, and you've always got to balance today against tomorrow. So if you sense your opportunity, go after it, no questions. Just do it carefully, and know that it may head-fake you, or drop you off somewhere you didn't exactly need to go to college for. Like back at your parent's house.

More people do it than you think, though, and start a lot of great things in garages they don't own. Still, you might also want to hold down a steady gig in the meantime. You know, just so you don't get stuck doing chores again.

10

The Money Will Make You Happy

> **When I was young I used to think money was the most important thing in life; now that I am old, I know it is.**
>
> —Oscar Wilde, being ironical

Lie no. 76
The Money Will Make You Happy

Our favorite tell-it-like-it-is mag, *Fast Company*, with its millennial survey a few years back, found most corporateers feel that money is the biggest deal in determining their success, their satisfaction, and their ability to live the kind of life they want to. Then the editors turn around and say people "are not altogether comfortable with the habits of acquisitiveness and consumerism—or even the drive to make more money."

Fellow publisher of the now-defunct *Spy* magazine, Kurt Andersen, pulls a page out of the Taoist bible to explain it, pointing to a cultural tug-of-war: "Money-grubbing and idealism are the yin and yang of the American soul," he feels, "perpetually coexisting." Which is just another way of saying we're all full of shit.

Most people don't grow up rolling in it, and can't help but believe the privileged are happier—because that's what people always believe. (Rich people even think that of the

> " Ambition is so powerful a passion in the human breast, that however high we reach, we are never satisfied. "
>
> —Niccolò Machiavelli, talking like Prince did about his mom in "When Doves Cry"

middle-class, but they're not about to sign the trust fund over to Jerry's Kids to find out.) Anyway, in spite of all the "more money, more problems" rap songs, workers need to see for themselves. And when they do land that $100K job—faster than they think—lo and behold, they wind up doing psychotherapy, retail therapy, or drug therapy. Maybe couples therapy, too, if they can catch it before he sleeps with the babysitter.

Not to be dramatic—and not to romanticize poverty—but you should know up front that the cash will only get you so far. More is usually better than less, granted; but there's a point of diminishing returns (see, econ wasn't a total waste), where more is just more, and doesn't let you do or buy anything that makes you any happier for any length of time. Including cars, clothes, and Jack & Cokes.

Because those kinds of things get old in time, and just sort of blend in with all the other stuff you've got. Then you go throw them away or trade-in, and see if it won't be different with this next round. Which it never is.

Sweating with the Joneses

"People find that their demands from life keep pace with their increases in income," explains Daniel Kahneman, Nobel Prize recipient for playing matchmaker with the fields of economics and psychology.

As a result, he says, everybody's on the so-called "satisfaction treadmill"—meaning that we want more fulfillment from the world as we earn more money, but don't really end up getting anywhere.

Great, the one piece of exercise equipment most people are willing to get on only makes your happiness thinner.

But a real relationship. Now, that eventually loses its new car smell, too; yet one of those, it turns out, can make you smile forever. Just so long as you're home often enough to keep it.

Lie no. 77
Cash Now, Dreams Later

As a newbie, chances are you don't have to worry about stinking up that new car with Taco Bell drive-thru; don't have to neatly throw away the wrappers in your three-bed, two-bath home; don't have much choice but to stick to the 99-cent menu; and don't really have very good prospects for changing that anytime soon. And don't forget to say thanks.

They don't call them *trappings* of success for nothing, where leases and mortgages and families (the kind you make, not the kind you move away from) all anchor you to this high-responsibility, high-stress, high-on-meth lifestyle you've bought into. And you've just got way too many changes to go through and mistakes to make before you get into all that. Start looking into it, I'd say, after your first or second divorce, at the earliest.

Until then, do like MBA guru Mark Albion says and "keep your walking costs low." In

> There is…an immeasurable distance between late and too late.
>
> —Anne Swetchine, for every guy who was just about to approach that girl…until *he* did first

other words, go month-to-month with the apartment, stay out of Ethan Allen, hang on to your beater Honda, and don't even dump the full 15 percent into your 401(k). Your dream job—or at least your next job—may be cross-state, cross-country, or even cross-cultured. And it's not so easy to head over the river and through the woods when you've got to put the house on the market, and need to find someone to take over the bargain $399/mo. lease on your 3-Series.

There's plenty of time for all that after your stomach gets a little flabbier, and you start passing out before ten—on the weekends. Right now you should be worried about sucking all the marrow you can out of life's bones, and being accountable to as few people and institutions as possible. Your family and educational lenders are more than enough.

And not only for the *carpe diem,* do-it-while-you-can bit, but because you'll start to get comfortable, and not want to give up all the pretty, breakable things you've managed to surround yourself with. So you have to do your best to resist the I'll-just-do-this-for-a-while-and-make-some-money-and-get-out mentality, because you probably won't. Or by the time you do, you'll have lost the energy and freshness to really put behind whatever's next. Instead, you'll just be spent and jaded and made fun of by the grunts you hire. In short, you'll become your boss.

You're too young to get comfortable, anyway, and should've learned from watching your parents how stupid it is to get into something you don't like (jobs *and* marriage). Just keep it cheap and disposable for now, until you really find what you're looking for. Like furniture.

An Offer He Couldn't Refuse

"People are shocked to hear that I think of *The Godfather* series with sadness," confesses Academy Award-winning film-maker Francis Ford Coppola. "I see those films almost as a personal failure."

Instead of Corleone, it seems he would've much rather it had been *Annie Hall*: "Their success led me to make big commercial films—when what I really wanted to do was original films, like those that Woody Allen is able to focus on."

Lie no. 78
Executives Are Really Important People

CEOs get almost as much press as celebrities and athletes nowadays. In part, I'm sure, because so many of them are on trial. And to watch them on the stand, most are better actors than whoever NBC has got on "Must See TV."

That said, the question to ask is why are we so fascinated with all these old, pudgy white men? (Even the ones who haven't fleeced their shareholders.) Which isn't discounting their accomplishments, to be sure; it takes a lot of smarts and hard work and golf with people you don't like to get to the top, and I applaud them. But what are we really celebrating here?

Is it out of respect, or out of fear they'll lay us off? Maybe it's a father-figure thing. Or perhaps watching them play Pac-Man with competitors and win corporate pissing contests is the aphrodisiac—getting us all lathered up over a power that most of us can only exercise over house-trained dogs and shy lovers.

> " We must believe in luck. For else how can we explain the success of those we don't like? "
>
> —Jean Cocteau, forgetting we can at least feel better about it by slashing their tires

Whatever the case, it sells a lot of newspapers and magazines. Some to me. Which are an interesting read, and important to stay current with, and all that; but let's keep it straight here.

Nothing that these guys do—again, except for the really bad stuff that costs lots of folks their jobs—is all that consequential in the bigger picture. Certainly, some businesses have a massive cultural and lifestyle influence (e.g., Starbucks, iPods, Google, Trojans), but you've got to keep that separate from the people themselves. Especially insofar as this is something you're aspiring to do or be one day.

Because apart from the Martin Luther Kings and Mother Teresas that come along every few generations, people aren't out there changing humanity on a grand scale—including big-time company officers. With the rare exception of icons like Bill Gates and Donald Trump, nobody's going to remember anything these

A Bunch of Gap

Our man Mark Albion got into executive coaching after leaving Harvard, and found himself on the phone with Mickey Drexler, CEO of Gap, Inc. at the time.

"Mr. Drexler," he asked, "what if the Gap disappeared tomorrow? Who other than your employees would really care? I mean, why is the Gap important? What does it *really* stand for?"

This was their first conversation. And, needless to say, their last. But he's got a pretty good point when you think about it: How big a deal is selling jeans, in the grand scheme of things?

I'm wearing a pair of their boot-cut low-rises right now, don't get me wrong; but let's not get carried away either. We all know that what really matters is what happens after you take them off.

people did two, three years from now. And would you really say that putting Windows on every office desk in the world is on par with civil rights? (In this particular case, it's probably closer to the other way around.)

Which shows you that values are relative—that no matter how big it seems, it's still just your little corner of the world. So you'd better love it for real, because better than 99 percent of corporate hotshots never get to see their name in the *Wall Street Journal.* And even if they do, it's usually in most recycle bins by mid-afternoon.

That, and Another Drink

"Money's easy to make, if it's money you want. But with few exceptions, people don't want money. They want...love and admiration."

—John Steinbeck

Lie no. 79
Money Says a Lot about You

Like we do with really attractive people, we equate having money with having all sorts of other wonderful attributes. But then you look at someone like Jerry Springer or Don King, and that theory gets shot right to hell, doesn't it? Throw Britney Spears into the mix, and you can kill both ideas at once.

Same thing holds for company execs pulling down seven, often eight figures a year after bonuses. Which I'm not necessarily criticizing—especially if the organization is keeping tens of thousands of employees on the payroll, helping to make sure the kids get the new *Grand Theft Auto* game for Christmas this year, and can have some fun carjacking and murdering innocent characters. But, again, you've got to separate the pay from the people, and ask yourself what that fat Benz in the assigned parking spot really represents (besides a monthly payment bigger than your rent).

So it's instructive, I think, to consider the individuals who did nothing to

> 66 **Many a small thing has been made large by the right kind of advertising.** 99
>
> —Mark Twain, and this was before under-endowed guys bought Porsches

> **❝ I'm living so far beyond my income that we may almost be said to be living apart. ❞**
>
> —E.E. Cummings, who couldn't even afford to capitalize

get the money they have except for getting born. And by looking at the Paris Hiltons of the world and pinching the bridge of your nose, it becomes a lot easier to see what kind of statement you're working so hard to make.

Here in its most passive form, what does money really say about a person? Far as I can tell, it's little more than "thank you, Daddy!" If you ever saw that documentary on HBO, *Born Rich,* the main distinction between us and them is that they can outspend and under-think everyone, and be incredibly obnoxious doing it. In fact, you could probably rerun the film on PBS—as a seventy-five-minute public service announcement for keeping kids off of cash.

Not that the next-of-kin all have their fingers up their noses, either, but the point is pretty clear: The money doesn't mean anything if there's no passion or purpose in making it. In just the same way that these hand-me-down-rich aren't necessarily any happier (and certainly no smarter) for their bloodline, high-paid execs aren't always any happier for their business cards. Many times, in fact, they're just as scared and desperate as the kids who have to use an intercom to figure out if Mom or Dad are home.

So, once again, you'd better love the work, and not just for what it does to your monthly statement from Citibank. Because whomever you're trying to impress, it's not happening. And that's not what a career is supposed to be about, anyway. Your job should be a statement about what's important to you; not what's important to Corporate America or high society. Unless those two value sets happen to meet on their own, and for the right reasons.

Which doesn't include love, by the way, if that's what you think the expensive bottle of wine at dinner is going to get you...

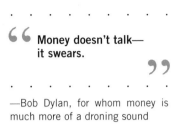

Money doesn't talk—it swears.

—Bob Dylan, for whom money is much more of a droning sound

Lie no. 80
You Can Have It All

Nobody has it all. *Nobody*. Especially the people who look like they do. Maintaining that kind of image is generally the work of really good PR and really good pharmaceuticals. The people who have it together best, in fact, are usually the ones you can find breaking down from time to time (hopefully not in front of clients). At least they're being straight with themselves—if not the company—about how tough it is to be successful at a job and a life all at once.

At this point in your career, you often have to choose between the two, and that's okay for a little while. (Plus you've probably got the stamina and liver capacity to pull off both when you need to.) But bigger picture, after you run out of gas, it's critical that you're thinking about how you want to play the family versus work game. I mean, you're not going to know for sure until you make it there, obviously; but you can at least start asking yourself today what's more important to you: Driving the luxury

> 66 To be unhappy at home is the ultimate result of all ambition. 99
>
> —Samuel Johnson, who I think married his job instead of his girlfriend

SUV to the office on a Saturday, or packing the kids and some sandwiches into the Toyota and heading to the beach instead?

Wouldn't you know it, here comes economics again: The scarce resource here is *time,* and you've got to figure out the most profitable way to invest it. Because this isn't the kind of decision you want to just let collect interest on

> ❝ I have yet to hear a man ask for advice on how to combine marriage and a career. ❞
>
> —Gloria Steinem, probably because it would give her too much satisfaction

its own. That's where custody battles and frequent-flyer miles and hypertension come from, and none of those things should be accidental. Not unless you think you've got a real shot at meeting Scarlett Johansson in some kind of *Lost in Translation* moment.

And what breadwinners stuck in foreign countries claim to be doing "for the children" is often the worst thing they could pick. Which you've got to sympathize with, to some extent, because who doesn't want to give their loved ones all the best things? It's just that the best thing, usually, is showing up to the soccer match, and not the imported toy you buy to say sorry. Although there wouldn't even be a soccer match if the money wasn't there to pay the league dues. So what's the answer then?

Listen, if I could tell you that, I'd be writing a different kind of book. All I know is that it's a really hard thing to do, and that you've got to find some way to do it. Everybody wants a successful career and a successful family and a successful home and a successful golden retriever and all that. But the reality of the situation is that something's got to give. And it's usually either your job, your family, or your body. Only one of which, as we already know, you can bounce back from.

So I guess it comes back to values, doesn't it? Maybe career is most important to you today, whereas in ten years it might be going to Hawaii with the rugrats. Or maybe it'll always be a corner-office thing with you, who knows? It's ultimately your decision to make. Just be sure it's you making it, and not the guy who's signing your paychecks. Because at the end of a long day, only one of you is going home to the warm embrace of your loving spouse. (I hope.)

Lie no. 81
The Safe Move Is a Safe Move

The National Association of Colleges and Employers conducted a big survey recently to figure out what kids were doing after graduation, besides eating Lucky Charms in their underwear. Rounding out the top five, in order, were: sales, management trainee, teaching, accounting, and finance.

Teaching I can see, but the rest? Nobody cared about any of that. I mean, tell me the last time you saw a campus rally organized to protest a new FASB standard. Or got a flyer for "Closing Skills Awareness Week."

Hard-reality-of-life thing again? Yep, Dad was right. But only to an extent: If you're taking one of these button-down jobs because you really feel like it'll be a great learning experience, and will help you beef-up the résumé for the next step toward the Big Dream, then

But There's No Final...

"Xers are the most likely to agree that they'd be willing to 'work at a boring job as long as the pay was good,'" reads a recent report from Yankelovich Partners, Inc.

Which is sad, but not altogether surprising. After all, it wasn't that long ago you were willing to sit through a poke-your-eyeballs-out class if it was an easy A.

Difference today is that the semester lasts a year or more; the course generally goes past fifty minutes a day; you don't meet just on Tuesdays and Thursdays; and it's not so easy to drop if you change your mind.

Well, Too Late Now...

Richard Leider, a thirty-year career counselor and author of several books, has spent a good deal of his professional life hanging out with the geriatric set; you know, looking at pictures of grandkids, eating dinner at 4:30, that sort of thing.

So what have interviews with more than one thousand senior citizens taught him about making the days count? "Remarkably," Leider says, "I hear the same answer. The good life means living in the place where you belong, being with the people you love, doing the right work—on purpose."

On balance, our elders wish they would've taken more risks, been more reflective, not have worried about money so much. Almost none of them, it seems, can really remember their days in the office (or what they wore yesterday). What they do recall, though, are times spent with family and friends: talking, traveling, playing, getting drunk and freaky.

Life only moves faster after fifty, so you'd better get to it now. You'll be gumming tapioca pudding sooner than you think.

great. We all need to get grounded in the principles of Big Business at some point, and sooner is usually better than later. But if this is one of those, "Oh shit, I'm graduating next month and I don't know how I'm going to pay my loans back," then that's another story.

And usually the more common of the two. But you can't be so sloppy anymore. Yet you also can't play it so safe: Now's the time, as you know, to go stick your pinky toe in the water, and to not get all caught up in the big, heavy lifestyle. So if you ever wanted to go join Greenpeace, or teach English in Japan, or fetch coffee and get belittled on a movie set, go do it today. Because when junior needs school clothes or a pipe bursts in the house, you can't very well pick up and go to cooking school in Paris at that point.

If you've got to move home or live on Top Ramen, then that's what you've got to do. But for God sake, go make it happen *now,* whatever it is. As Grandma and Grandpa remind us, you only get so many chances to do it right—but a whole lifetime to think about all the chances you missed.

Remember, Corporate America will always be there, and will always be hiring, somewhere. Only take the job at this point if it really makes sense for your big career vision. Otherwise, you should be out there making as little sense as possible.

Lie no. 82
You'll Wish You Spent More Time at the Office

I'm going to get a little morbid again, but it's true that none of us really know the expiration date on our packages.

Thanks to that work-in-progress, modern medicine, we've been able to add more years to life. But for all of the advances, we've yet to figure out how to add more life to our years—and there's no drug for that.

So as a newbie with more than two-thirds of your days still in front of you—and the advice of those with more than two-thirds of theirs behind them—you're in a pretty good position to get what you want out of this world. Provided you get out of the office on time most weeks.

Towers Fall, Dreams Rise

The attacks of September 11th shook all of us in this country, some more powerfully than others. And less talked about, not all for the worse.

Enlistment inquiries at the U.S. Marine Corps, for instance, soared more than 400 percent; the American Red Cross, in just half a month, registered more than 160,000 hits to its website; applications at fire departments across the country were filed at unprecedented rates.

Not that these are the right moves for everyone—or even for these people—but it was at least driven by a real sense of purpose. And some kids finally grew up to become firemen…

Enough dead poets and politicians have reminded us that history is a broken record (outdated expression, but I like it), and you could easily still piss away most of your life breathing in refrigerated air if you're not careful. So instead of reiterating the reiterated, I'll just remind you again that you could bite it at any point.

Including at the start of your "golden years," if your plan is to save up all the good stuff for retirement. You never know what kind of situation—physical, mental, financial—you or your part-

ner might be in. And then there went all those years of sacrifice for a bum knee, an RV you can't drive, an empty IRA account, and a permanently limp member because of his heart medication.

Plus you've also got to think about what you want to look back on your life and see when you're in the rocking chair, asking people to repeat themselves. Because what it really comes down to is memories; which ones are going to keep you company when maybe

> **66 Most of us go to our graves with our music still inside us. 99**

—Oliver Wendell Holmes, who unfortunately wasn't talking about Michael Bolton

nobody else is there to. And the last thing you want to die with (other than a colostomy bag, perhaps) is regrets.

Really, it's like Ferris Bueller reminded us: Life moves pretty fast, and if you don't stop and look around once in a while, you could miss it. After all, you only get so much time to create your life's meaning. And you only get so many days off.

11

Don't Worry, the Company Will Take Care of You

> 66 If you pick up a starving dog and make him prosperous, he will not bite you. This is the principal difference between a dog and a man. 99

—Mark Twain, and also between a dog and a company. Even starving ones you come in on the weekends for.

Lie no. 83
There's Still a Ladder to Climb

Even if there were still a ladder, why would you want to be on it? I mean, sure, there's something to be said for stability, security, sensible shoes, all this—and that something is usually, "Oh, thanks, that's really sweet; but I prefer to date musicians."

Lucky for you, you're not allowed to be that boring anymore. Or at least not as predictable, in part because companies aren't either. It used to be that they could offer you a nice, safe thirty-year trip up the rungs, and actually mean it. There was a kind of social compact in place, where if you agreed to a solid 9-to-5, the boss would let you get home in time for meatloaf with your two-and-a-half kids. Which, in truth, was a much easier way to live, provided you could deal with the golly-gosh-gee-whiz of it all.

In today's business environment, however, that social compact is lining the bird's

Same Ol,' Same Ol'

According to Right Management Consultants' 2004 Career Confidence Index, nearly one in three American workers is pretty confident that they're not going anywhere in their current workplace. Besides out.

And this consulting group, incidentally, is the one companies call when those one out of three were correct: They're in the "outplacement" business, or finding fired workers new jobs. Nice racket, huh?

cage: With all the advances in technology, the growing Made-in-Bangalore issue, along with rising healthcare costs for a workforce that's not going gray very gracefully, it's much more of a let's-wait-and-see-what-happens kind of thing. Corporate America has become the guy who won't take you ring shopping.

Which is fine, because once again, business, like Utah, isn't the place for monogamy. You're exclusive while you're in something, definitely, but never so committed that you don't get slapped occasionally for your wandering eye. And not that you go dangling one foot out the door, either. On the contrary, when you're in it, you need to be *in it;* no fantasizing about other managers during your meetings. That'll start to come through in your work, and then nobody's going to get what they need out of the relationship.

Instead, you keep doing the best job you can do, and decide from time to time if this is still the best job you can be doing. Which isn't to say that you might not have a solid five or seven year stretch somewhere—a

---

Peter's Principle

"The stepladder is gone, and there's not even the implied structure of an industry's rope ladder. It's more like vines, and you bring your own machete," explains management sherpa Peter Drucker in the vaunted *Harvard Business Review.*

"It is time to give up thinking of jobs or career paths as we once did and think in terms of taking on assignments, one after the other."

By the way, our man Peter said this more than a decade ago, back in 1993. So glad we were all listening.

place where you can really dig in and kick ass and learn a ton. But, inevitably, that learning plateaus, and the only place you have to go from there is bored.

. . . .

❝ There is no security on this earth. Only opportunity.

❞

. . . .

—General Douglas MacArthur, who was in the security business

So if you're all ra-ra-sis-boom-ba about a company right now, great; you'll both benefit from it as long as you can keep it up. But don't hang on longer than you should because you're scared or that's what Dad did. In fact, Dad probably did it *because* he was scared, and that's almost never a good reason to do anything. Including becoming a dad.

As bad management philosophies go, this one isn't so bad: "management by exception." What I like about it is that it's intuitive—you figure out what works by seeing what doesn't. And it's also self-correcting, because you know right away when something (or someone) has stopped doing its job.

What I like most about the theory, though, is that it works even better for careers: You figure out the kind of work you like by hating most of it. And quite a start you're off to already, huh?

Practically speaking, though, that means doing some damage to the résumé, in a couple of ways: First off, you have to be willing to boogie from job to job until you get it right, which might take some explaining to recruiters. We'll chat more about this toward the end of the chapter, but so long as we're not talking three

Screw You Guys, I'm Going Home!

According to the U.S. Bureau of Labor Statistics, the average American holds 8.6 jobs between the ages of eighteen and thirty-two, and the median length of time workers stay in one position has been cut in half since 1983—from 2.2 years back then to around 1.1 years in 2003.

So don't get too comfy, wherever you are. You've got a lot more company sweatshirts to collect and wash the car with.

Keep On Keepin' On

"During one's twenties and thirties, the only way to assess oneself is to take different jobs in different companies to find out what kind of work one does best, enjoys most, and finds most meaningful," conclude our friends Bartolomé and Evans in that peach of a *Harvard Business Review* study, "Must Success Cost So Much?"

"Our research indicates," they continue, "that foreclosing this phase of exploration too quickly may have negative consequences later in one's career."

Like becoming that amazingly boring girl at the party nobody wants to talk to. C'mon, toughen up and call a headhunter already!

weeks here, month-and-a-half there, a good backstory will usually do the trick.

The harder part here, really, is when it comes time to taking one of those no-name, high-risk, or even Plain Jane gigs. Because while the Fortune 500 can well be a respectable and recognizable place to earn your keep, it's not always the right place to keep earning it.

Don't get me wrong; there are some wicked smart people in these organizations, and you can get exposed to some very high-level stuff very early on. (From a safe distance, anyway.) But some of the best education you'll ever get will be with a small company—a startup, a little niche shop, a family-run business—a place where you can see ins and outs, and where people really know what you do there. Which is perhaps the biggest risk of this kind of job.

Not that this is right for everyone, and not that it's right right away. But should you find yourself in front of a building that doesn't have a big, sexy name on it—

or a big, sexy paycheck to go with—don't reflexively turn away. If you want it, then you do it, no matter what side of the tracks it's on (like love). Because your résumé should be an explanation of your experience; never a reason for it.

Besides, there's a mob of research out there showing that the people who are most satisfied with their careers today are doing something they never planned on earlier in their lives. So, go ahead, get in bed with whoever you want. Just remember that rich girls have morning breath, too.

So You're Saying There's a Chance...

"The probability that the first choice you make is right is roughly one in a million. If you decide your first choice is the right one, chances are you are just plain lazy."

—Peter Drucker

Lie no. 85
You Only Get One Career

Nobody has just one career anymore. Including pro athletes, who usually have business interests outside of the game. Because even their bloated salaries aren't enough to cover tuition for all those illegitimate children.

But you, with the normal height and libido. There's no telling how many things you'll end up doing before you start putting your grandkids to sleep—going on about all the things you ended up doing.

And I don't mean jobs; you'll go through those like Madonna does images. Like Snoop Dogg does joints and mispronunciations. No, I mean *careers:* completely new gigs in completely new fields.

Especially with how the market is today—and your guess is nearly as good as

Spice of Life

"Futurists predict that Millennials will experience as many as ten career changes in their lifetimes. That's *career* changes, not *job* changes," or so says that doozy of a management book, *When Generations Collide.*

Assuming you live to eighty-two, start working at twenty-two, and never retire, that's a new career every six years.

Now, either these futurists have got their imaginary numbers wrong, or everyone in Gen Y is going to be a renaissance man. Or a flake.

Plan on around five. Seven max. Just like marriages.

Alan Greenspan's about what tomorrow's will look like—you might find yourself serving drinks on flights to the moon just as soon as you find yourself serving on the Ninth Circuit Court of Appeals.

Anyway, point is that even if you know where you're going, you don't. Which is a pretty exciting idea—that the potential's there for you to do or be something you're not even aware exists right now. Perhaps it'll even be your fault it exists. Or maybe you'll just end up in jail like your uncle, who can tell?

Whatever the case, don't get too married to whatever you're doing for a living

right now. (Like I have to sell that one to you.) You'll be happy to know that many of the skills and experiences you're gaining are totally transferable to whatever's next, because it's *all* business. So just keep building and growing and readying yourself, and then move when it's time to move. You can't be this uptight forever.

Repeat Daily, with a Parachute

"I am essentially a 'temp' worker, hunting for a job whose length I do not know. I am going to have to be mentally prepared to start job hunting again, at any time."

—Richard Nelson Bolles

Lie no. 86
The Company Will Keep You During Lean Times

When things get bad, if you don't own the place, your job isn't safe. Especially if you're part of an overhead department, like marketing, which spends the money that divisions like sales and engineering bring in. Those are the first guys to go. Then you'll see broader cuts through the middle: project managers, account managers, division managers, hopefully your manager. Finally, if they're really in a spot, you'll see them start to pick off some of their own, changing the locks on the executive washroom just to be sure.

As a grunt, it's hit or miss: You're completely expendable if need be, but you're cheap, too. So sometimes they'll keep you around if they think you can step up and be even more underpaid. Which isn't always a bad thing to be when it's ugly everywhere else, and people

Job Security (You Mean Like Funny "Ha Ha"?)

Think you've got it tough? Try being a suit-and-tie guy in the early '90s:

- Sears Roebuck mowed down fifty thousand employees.
- AT&T reached out and fired forty thousand.
- IBM formatted a whopping sixty-three thousand nerds from payroll.

—From *The Working Life*

with Wharton MBAs are doing temp gigs for $15 or $20 an hour.

Where I'm going with this is that you can't get too comfortable or too cocky where you are, because you might not be there as long as you think. Really, you're just a few cents a share below projected earnings from having the federal government subsidize your next visit to Monster.com.

So what to do about it? Nothing, except be ready: With this scenario in the back of your mind, you should be aggressively working the organization for all of the skills, experience, and contacts you can muster. Which isn't a bad or mercenary thing, because it just means you're adding that much more value to the company. Remember, what's good for you is *great* for them, and usually by at least a 25 percent profit margin.

Which also means that when there's nothing left on the table, you have to be just as ready to pick up and foot them with the bill, as we talked about. Like any relationship, it stops being a good deal once they're getting much more out of it than you are. Although that definitely does take some time, so you can't be too hasty about flipping them the bird, either.

Still, when you know it's over, it's generally easier to dump them first. Then there's less fighting over computer files and albums and dishes and stuff.

See Honey, Sometimes Faster Is Better...

The U.S. Bureau of Labor Statistics crunched out another good one: By their count, job seekers between the ages of twenty-five and thirty-four were unemployed for an average of sixteen weeks during 2003.

So try to keep about four months worth of cash on hand at any time. Or at least a friend with a pull-out sofa.

Lie no. 87
Getting Laid Off Is a Big Deal

L ots of really successful people have been laid off, and today say it's one of the best things that ever happened to them—including Michael Bloomberg (now the mayor of NYC), Jessie "The Body" Ventura (pro wrestler who was also, inexplicably, the governor of Minnesota), Bernie Marcus (founder of Home Depot), Larry King (talk-show host with the suspender fetish), and even Muhammad Ali.

Some of that's wishful thinking, of course, because I'm sure they would've done these great things on their own at some point; the firing was just a kick in the ass. Which was otherwise coming from their wives, no doubt.

No, the real story here is that losing a position has nothing to do with losing your pride or your courage or your girlfriend. Because really smart and talented

A Firing by Any Other Name...

Terminated, canned, laid off, axed, booted, sacked, downsized, made redundant—call it what you will. Same thing. Except, somehow, when they say it...

Xerox:

"Involuntary force reductions"

Sun Oil:

"Managing down staff resources"

Executive firings:

"Pursuing other interests"

—From *The Way We Talk Now* ("Other interests," by the way, often include seeing the kids and calling them by the right names.)

people—way more smart and talented than you and me, or at least me—get handed their walking papers all the time.

Sure, as you'd guess, they get angry and hurt and depressed and go get a few drinks to make it all better. But once they're done taking it personally, they realize that this was much more about the company than them. One of the only times, in fact, where the "it's not you, it's me" line isn't complete bollocks.

Lesser of Two Evils

A 2004 report by research firm Rainmaker Thinking found that college graduates ages twenty to twenty-four faced a jobless rate of around 10 percent, while workers twenty-five to thirty-four were just shy of 6 percent.

Companies have a tough choice: pay more in salaries, or pay more in mistakes and attitude. And you can see which way they're leaning...

Because corporations, on the whole, are embarrassingly mismanaged; the bigger the worse. So they get liberal with the checkbook during the upswings, and then wake up with a hangover when the market turns. At which point the mandate comes down that they've got to "tighten their belts" and operate "lean and mean" and whatever other way PR wants to spin it. Bottom line is that your department is now on the chopping block.

Meaning you're the one who's going to end up paying for their boondoggles and failed initiatives, and there's nothing you can do about it. Except get up and shake it off.

Hey, it paid your school loans and gave you free high-speed Internet access while it lasted—and you might even get a decent little severance package out of it, too. Including, sometimes, help finding your next gig. So put away the hard feelings, because none of this was about you. Not to them, anyway.

That's business for ya, and you'd better get used to it. It takes thick skin and a good attitude to make it, so toughen up and smile. You'll get laid again.

Generally speaking, you should put about as much of yourself into your job as you did into your college major. Even though you may not change your job as often.

Until it's your own business, and even then, work is something you *do;* not someone you *are*. Which can be a difficult concept for recent grads—many of whom referred to their school as "we" and "us" in conversation, and coordinated their wardrobe around the university color palette.

Now, ideally there are important parts of your character and personality that come through in your job—like how naturally you clear paper jams from the printer, and come up with on-the-fly excuses for irate clients. But no matter how well the company "gets you," there should always be a clear separation between work-life and life-life. Even

What's the Hang-Up?

A recent telephone survey of one thousand people (during dinner, I'm sure) by the Yale School of Management revealed that nearly one in four workers are chronically angry at the office.

Most often because employers "violated basic promises," and didn't fulfill the "expected psychological contract with their workers."

So I guess that pisses off girlfriends *and* employees...

if that life-life doesn't have an answering machine that goes blink-blink.

Which, if it doesn't, is really your fault, as we already covered when talking about finding your (im)balance. And this is also different from having a career that's grounded in your values and priorities; you're still doing that, too, or obviously should be. The point here is that even while all this is going on, there still has to be a "you" that's distinct from whatever this "you" happens to be doing for a living right now. At least that's what the Backstreet Boys keep telling themselves.

You might lose a job you really love later on, or go through a management change that f's the whole place up. How are you going to cope when you're only home to check the mail and pass out? Which doesn't mean, either, that you don't put your heart and soul into your work when it's appropriate; you just can't leave them there

Open Relationship

"Of all the institutions in society, why would we let one of the more precarious ones supply our social, spiritual, and psychological needs?" asks Joanne Ciulla in *The Working Life.*

It's a good question, Joanne. Although I'm not sure companies are doing anything spiritually, other than causing workers to periodically take the Lord's name in vain.

"It is important for people to be connected to activities and organizations unrelated to work," she continues. "If they lose or change their jobs, they'll have other friends, communities, and interests to support them."

And it's not like you're getting that much support to begin with from someone who's got their eye on your cube...

after the project's done. No different than classes and hookups back in school.

So do your best to keep your distance and keep busy elsewhere. Businesses come and go, don't forget, and it's not like they're giving you some great college experience or sports program to get all passionate about. And even if they did, the football team would probably suck anyway.

> " I like long walks, especially when they are taken by people who annoy me. "
>
> —Fred Allen, for no reason whatsoever

Lie no. 89
Get Close to Your Coworkers

ame college rules apply here: You should get about as close to your coworkers as you did whomever you sat next to in lecture. At least those friendships were honest—where you talked only when you were there, mostly about how stupid the professor was, and felt no need to stay in touch after the semester was over. If only all breakups were that clean.

Which is entirely separate and apart from having a laugh in the office with your cubemates, and maybe the occasional beer outside of it. And which also doesn't mean that there won't be a handful of people you meet throughout your career that become real, true, long-standing friends. It's just that most of them are much more likely to become real, true, longstanding idiots you'd otherwise have nothing to do with.

That may be overstating it. But there's absolutely a difference between the kinds of friends you have at work and the kinds of friends you have outside of it. And for good reason, because the

> 66 **Business entertaining is an oxymoron. It is neither business nor is it entertaining.** 99
>
> —Judith Martin, "Miss Manners" herself (Even she's entitled to an off-day once in a while, I suppose.)

two don't go together: You're never competing against a college buddy or someone on an intramural softball team, after all, for a promotion—and those precious little whisper-and-giggle conversations you have never get leaked to someone with a financial stake in your comings and goings.

Plus, same issue as knocking boots with your colleagues—what happens if one of you moves into a reporting position? It'd be kind of tough, I imagine, to have those bitching sessions with the person you're actually bitching about: "Oh, and when you said that during the meeting, I was thinking to myself, 'How in the hell did she ever get this job?' It was classic!"

It's an interesting dynamic, and one you have to handle carefully. On the one hand, your opportunities to meet other people are limited, and you do get to know and feel comfortable with your coworkers pretty quickly. On the other hand, how much do you really

Difference Being...?

Hurting for some more business insight into your world? Thought so. Try this one on:

The Eight Key Values of the Twentysomething Generation

- They are self-oriented.
- They feel cynical.
- They are materialistic.
- Their adolescence is extended.
- They want quality time.
- They want to have fun.
- They are slow to commit.
- They don't bow to authority.

—From *Twentysomething: Managing and Motivating Today's New Workforce*

(And how this separates newbies from anyone else in the office, don't ask me.)

have in common apart from hating everyone else in the department? And isn't looking at this person's mug for upwards of ten hours a day enough for you?

People do it all the time, though—dinner, drinks, S&M clubs after work—and being social like that is generally healthy. Plus, once in a while, some genuine stuff can come out of these things (for women, typically, more so than men). Just be selective with where, when, how much, and definitely who: There's a difference, after all, between having a pal when you can't leave someplace before 6 p.m. and when you can.

66 **Never cut what you can untie.**

99

—Joseph Joubert, except for failed relationships. There's no such thing as "just friends" after second base.

So if you feel that calling them up to hang out on a weekend won't make things weird (or just redundant), then try it out. But if things turn work-related, put the kibosh on that quick. No good can come of it professionally or personally. Besides, what will you have left to gripe about on Monday?

Lie no. 90
Quit When It Gets Bad

A little bad isn't always so bad. Tough times at work put hair on your chest, let you know you're alive, make you look forward to better days. And for those of you who aren't particularly interested in the man-fur or the optimism, the fact is that sometimes you just can't quit without screwing yourself in the process.

We've already decided that the résumé isn't going to dictate your career path, and this definitely still holds. But if you're saying peace before a year's time, that does look a little suspicious to whoever's looking.

Job tenures continue to drop, and smart employers realize that someone who's bringing experience and perspective from a number of places is going to be that much more valuable. What

It Really *Is* a Rat Race

"Where am I more likely to find Cheese—here or in the Maze?" asks Spencer Johnson in his quirky little bestseller, *Who Moved My Cheese?*

Idea being, once they've taken "Yesterday's Cheese" away (i.e., the good stuff about a job), it's not coming back. So the question becomes, when do the risks of going back out into the Maze (i.e., the labor market) outweigh the stink of Today's Cheese?

When things really get funky: "Smell the Cheese often so you know when it's getting old," Spencer says. It's not always that easy to tell, of course, it being Cheese and all. Just don't wait until you're gagging.

they want to know is what happened: Who you pissed off, how you did it, why it couldn't be fixed, and when you think you might try that again here. The same kinds of questions you're asked, really, when you start getting serious with someone and finally have to have the "The Number" discussion. (The correct answer, by the way, is five for men, three for women. No more, no less. And you're welcome.)

> 66 **Work only tires a woman, but it ruins a man.** 99
>
> —African proverb, and the primary difference between mothers and fathers

If you tell them flatly that you just didn't like it there and wanted more money, while refreshingly honest—and what everyone is thinking—that's not an acceptable answer. They want to see some stick-with-it-ness; that you're not going to bail on them come crunch time. Especially at the beginning of your career, when there's no track record, you have to be fairly judicious about the kinds of moves you make and when you make them. A couple of quick early departures, and suddenly you're a flake, a floater, a high flight risk. That was for college.

Plus you don't know what you're missing out on. Of course, with the tension and the yelling and the shitwork you do; I'm talking about all the learning that comes with it. Throw away the first few months while you're still figuring everything out—and the few months after that when you're starting to get seriously drowsy—there's a lot that can still happen. It's sort of a threshold you need to cross, when you become a known entity and people start trusting you with stuff. Only after that does your political capital begin to build, and you can start to make things happen on your own.

So feel it out. If your instincts are saying that you're not going to make it (i.e., hurting yourself or others), then obviously get out of there. But if you're just bored, then you need to sack up and take it for a while, see where things go. If after another six months you still find yourself coming in late, leaving early, handing in sloppy work, missing meetings, getting more bold with your mouthing-off—then, yeah, update the résumé. At that point, you may need it sooner than you plan on.

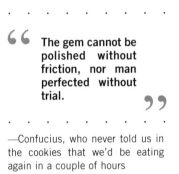

The gem cannot be polished without friction, nor man perfected without trial.

—Confucius, who never told us in the cookies that we'd be eating again in a couple of hours

But do try to make it at least a year. You don't want to explain a fling to anyone.

What's Wrong with What's Next

> **Man makes plans, God laughs.**

—Yiddish proverb (and the Yiddish are usually so upbeat, go figure)

To this point, it's always been pretty easy to say what's next, mostly because you haven't had a say. It was from one school to the following—perhaps in a different town, at your parents' discretion—call your grandmother, eat your lima beans, lights out by eleven, and you shouldn't be reading those kinds of magazines, mister.

Then college comes, your prison break. If you live on the West Coast, school's in the East. If you live on the East Coast, school's in the West. If you live in the Midwest, school's any-freakin'-where else. But between tuition, housing, and actual acceptance letters, your university still picked you more than the other way around.

> " By the criteria I used, self-actualization does not occur in young people. "
>
> —Abraham Maslow, whose "Hierarchy of Needs" you're at the bottom of (C'mon, you remember getting that one wrong on your intro psych midterm.)

No, your first real big life decision arrived when it came time to select a major. And what did you do? That's right, "undeclared." Well done, Mom and Dad were right about being able to trust you.

All that changed, of course, when your undergrad academic advisor forced you to finally choose something— but even then it was probably a throwaway, like psychology or something. (A field in which I'm a proud bachelor.)

And then after that, quietly, with next to no preparation whatsoever, you were faced with the Big One. Real life. And what did you do? That's right, move back home. Now Mom and Dad have to take back all that crap about trusting you.

But that's not exactly fair, either, because this is a lot of pressure to put on someone whose exposure to the real world consisted of some part-time summer work, maybe an internship, and a few trips to the dentist. How that's supposed to be a guiding light to your professional calling, don't ask me. That's not even a flashlight.

So as a newbie facing an unscripted forty-year block of time—for the first time—it's not uncommon to find yourself drinking the hard stuff by lunch on a Tuesday. You can't know what you want to do until you actually do it, and even if you like something, you may go back and forth a few times: What gets you all silly one day might seem blah the next, and a string of good months can be unexpectedly and dramatically followed by a stretch of deep introspection and confusion. Which is all unexpectedly and dramatically normal.

Be patient with yourself and be patient with the process. And screw anyone who's leaning hard on you to call the ball, including the folks. They're not going to kick you out, I promise, and you can't internalize their pressure. I mean, you'll never have a regular bowel movement again.

Cover Your Eyes during This Part, Dear

"The youth refuses to wait until, after long study, suffering and deprivation, his picture of men and things is completed."

—Fredrich Nietzsche, from *Human, All Too Human*

Even for those people who get an offer from their top company, and are ushered in with warm smiles and interesting work (all three of them), they're still lugging emotional baggage in the attaché.

Because the basic, but very new, stresses of office life naturally give rise to all sorts of questions and worries and adult acne: "Do I fit in here?" "Did I make the right decision?" "Could I even get hired by another company?" "Will they find out I was never really in Phi Beta Kappa?"

Don't worry; these fears and apprehensions are shared by practically everyone—especially those whose employers do background checks. (In which case maybe you should worry, depending.) Regardless, even more Harvard research—this time with less of a "duh" factor—

Everybody Hurts

Bartolomé and Evans are at it again with their *Harvard Business Review* study, "Must Success Cost So Much?" reminding us that "no matter how well this process of starting one's own career and finding one's professional identity goes, the individual will suffer from considerable tension and stress."

All right, maybe we didn't need a Harvard study to tell us that. Still, it's a good point to keep in mind for those of you who are doing the round-peg-in-the-round-hole thing right now. As anyone who's been married for a while will tell you, shapes can change.

has revealed that many people go through a kind of yearlong depression when making a big career switch: They don't get all weepy and stop using deodorant, necessarily, but do experience many of the same feelings of loss, confusion, sadness, and not wanting to do the dishes. Plus every hiccup at the office makes it seem like their decision was that much worse.

Which it might've been; Harvard's not saying these people were right in relocating the family and starting up with the fourteen-hour days. But it's probably more attributable to an acclimation and adjustment period, like any new relationship. Which, do note, can take a lot longer outside of college, seeing as the purpose now isn't to get out of it by June.

At this stage of the game, any dynamic that works out—or doesn't—isn't a bad one: You're at the bottom, you've got nowhere to fall. Starting over at this point is as easy as it gets, so your timing with figuring out that you don't want this kind of career couldn't be better. And it doesn't even have to wait until June anymore.

Besides, you can't know what's what, quite frankly, because you haven't been doing this long enough to have a sense of things. So to get yourself all worked up over something whose consequences you can't even determine—and which really won't matter for long anyway—makes even less sense than your manager usually does. Not to minimize your feelings, of course; feelings aren't right or wrong. Irrational and counter-productive, perhaps, but not wrong.

Just try to keep them in check by keeping every-thing in perspective, and let the rest of it go. I know you didn't make it through college like this. Your room-mate would've killed you.

> 66 **Yield and overcome.** 99
>
> —Taoist philosopher Lao-Tzu (Advice good enough, incidentally, to start a religion and direct oncoming traffic)

Lie no. 93
Everything Will Go According to Plan

Nothing goes according to plan. Even plans that come close to going according to plan usually don't come very close. And when it comes to careers, the only plan you can really go according to is not having one. At least that's the plan according to me.

Well, not entirely. You definitely have to have an idea of where you're going; in fact, it has to be a really smart and well-developed idea, driven by your values and passions. But after that, who knows?

Because opportunities and insights and chance encounters can't be scripted; there's no accounting for life, when it comes down to it. All you can do, really, is bend and twist and adjust in response—maybe in line with what you planned before, and maybe not. It all

Losing My Lunch

VH1 did an interview a while back with R.E.M. frontman Michael Stipe, who was talking about their groundbreaking 1991 video for "Losing My Religion."

The director, Tarsem Singh, originally had an elaborate plan for how the shoot would go. But after a day of filming, apparently nothing was turning out and tensions were mounting. What do you do?

As Stipe recalls, "So, he went into the bathroom, threw up a couple of times, and came out and said, 'Okay, we're doing it like this...'"

The result: Six MTV Video Music Awards, with a special shout-out to Pepto-Bismol.

depends on what you run into and uncover and figure out. Like that you love marketing or don't like being this far away from home or can't act.

If you play chess at all, this shouldn't be an unfamiliar concept to you: At any given point, you have to be thinking three or four moves ahead, or at least look like you are. But then your opponent, inevitably, does something you didn't anticipate, and you've got to redraw your three or four moves to account for it. (And make a face like you've got at least seven.) Now your plan looks nothing like the one you just had a second ago. Which won't look anything like the one you'll have in a second.

And you're going to lose plenty of games in between. So don't get all caught up in any one plan. Focus, instead, on the *process* of planning:

About Face, Soldier!

For someone who never wanted to do big movies, Francis Ford Coppola sure is good at it. During the filming of his gritty war story *Apocalypse Now*, in fact, his star Martin Sheen suffered a heart attack. (And this was well before Marty saw his paycheck for the *West Wing*.)

But instead of delaying or even scrapping the film, Francis simply pulled in a double and shot most of the material from behind.

"To keep going in a crisis, do a 180-degree turn," Coppola advises (this time literally). "Don't look for the secure solution. Don't pull back from the passion."

So you *do* love it, Francis! You big lug, you!

Leave a Light On

"Anybody who takes a five-year plan and puts it in the wastebasket after one year and does it over has to be a little nuts. And I've never seen a plan that didn't get better in that process."

—Chuck Knight, former CEO, Emerson Electric Co.

Not knowing the next step, per se, but knowing how you want to get there. That's how all the best careers and dates go.

Lie no. 94
Trial and Error Is a Bad Thing

What's so wrong with guessing? I mean, back in school when there were exams, this wasn't the same issue. But out here, especially when it comes to careers, there's no Scantron, no blue book, no TA to show a little leg to and get a few questions ahead of time.

Because life isn't that neat and tidy and tucked into the pants. And not that it should be (that look is *so* out). Which means as you run into decisions you've never had to make before (e.g., buy or lease, quit or want to die, move in together or slow down), you can look to others for examples and guidance. But, it really just comes down to your best gander. It works out or it doesn't, and then you have an idea of which way to go the next time this comes up

Everybody's in R&D

"Twentysomethings often feel that that the only means they have for navigating the seemingly endless choices looming ahead of them is trial and error," complain authors Robins and Wilner in *Quarterlife Crisis.* "Which is just a productive-sounding euphemism for guess-work."

But what's so bad about guesswork that we need to call it something else? (And "trial and error" doesn't sound any more fruitful, if you ask me.) That's how we learn—baby to adult. Plus isn't this how pharmaceutical companies make most of their money, er, discoveries?

(e.g., buy if you can afford it, quit even if you can't afford it, and wait until after your wedding, which not even your parents can afford).

You'd be amazed, in fact, at how many people—ten, twenty years your senior—are still sort of making it up as they go along. In all parts of their lives. And, again, not that anything's wrong with that. Some of this is simply the process of living and doing dumb stuff—which you can tell funny stories about later on. Ideally while being drunk and doing some more dumb stuff. The problem, rather, is not being reflective about how you got mixed up with all of this stupidity to begin with.

Which happens most often, it seems, with jobs: People wake up to careers they don't recognize all the time, wheedled into bed by a bigger paycheck or a better title or just "something different." Putting no more thought into it, before or afterward, than what they can buy now or brag about or the next stranger they can introduce themselves to the following morning.

Which is stupid in ways you don't want to tell stories about. So don't forget about the chess match; it's not just moving a piece here or there. There's a strategy to it, fuzzy as it may be, that's guided by both your passions and reality. But you can't just take random, one-off stabs at your dreams and expect to make it. That only works for Carson Daly.

It's kind of like how modern medicine keeps getting more modern: educated guesses, patients with nothing to lose, a scalpel in one hand, crossed fingers in the other, and a no-frills review board. Well, that and a boatload of malpractice insurance.

> ### And Do It While You Can
>
> "'What was the worst thing that could happen?' I would ask myself. If it didn't work out, I'd start again."
>
> —Dan Case, former CEO of Hambrecht and Quist, prior to passing of cancer at forty-four

Lie no. 95
Knowing What You Should Do Means Doing It

So let's say you've got your strategy all worked out, right down to the little speech you're going to give your parents. Now there's just the tiny little matter of actually doing it.

Everybody, for instance, has said to themselves at some point, "You know, I should really write a book about this." Some of us, obviously, meant it more than others. But the ratio of sayers to doers is roughly everybody to one. And a little lower than that for those who actually get published.

And still not much better for those who have far more realistic and sensible goals, like wanting to be president or date Heidi Klum. Nope, they'll have these wonderfully ambitious and purposeful career plans, and then settle for something like banking or sales or, um, writing books.

Crimson Scribe

Here's Harvard sticking its nose in things again: Turns out they did a class study sometime back about goals, and found that only about 3 percent of the students had written theirs down.

Wouldn't you know, twenty years later the same 3 percent were wealthier than the other 97 percent combined.

Author's note: I got this off of a cardboard cutout from a store. Seems pretty inflated, but I like the story...

But you can't be a nancy about going after your goals. All the meditation and planning and pennies in the wishing well won't get you any closer to your dreams after a certain point. And that point—not too soon, not too late, not the same for everyone—is the difference between being something, and always wanting to have been something. Except, in this case, a liar.

Write your goals and ideas down, or share them with (trusted) people, or do whatever works for you to get your head in order. And you've absolutely got to research the hell out of the career path you're thinking about. That may take care of it for you right there. But if you're still hot on moving forward, then shut up and just do it. Even if you have to quote sneaker ads in the process.

Kissing and Telling

"I have always lived my life by making lists—lists of people to call, lists of ideas, lists of companies to set up, lists of people who can make things happen," explains Richard Branson, flamboyant CEO of Virgin.

Never without a cheap, standard-sized school notebook to jot down his thoughts, Branson has filled an entire bookcase with scribble pads as he's built business after business using this technique.

"Each day I work through these lists," he continues, "and that sequence of calls propels me forward." Well, that and his fleet of commercial jetliners.

—From *Losing My Virginity*

You Damn Sissy!

"Then there's the whole idea that the real military genius is the one who can win without firing a shot. Like, the general is so strategic that the other guy just falls down from sheer lack of strategic advantage. I've never actually seen that happen," prods Stanley Bing in his brilliant work, *Sun Tzu Was a Sissy*. (Sun Tzu, if you recall, was the military advisor who wrote *The Art of War* some centuries back, which Stan rips a new one.)

"It's the overreliance on strategy, however, that makes Sun Tzu such a limp biscuit at this particular point in the history of the world." And he's right. Your dreams aren't happening because you think really hard about them; you've got to go *work* for them. (And never annoy Stanley Bing.)

Lie no. 96
It's All Going to Happen Fast

What you don't see on ESPN is that good poker players fold on as many as 90 percent of their hands. Doesn't mean they don't keep anteing up, or go all-in when they've got the right cards; but mostly it's just a lot of sitting around and waiting for the right bet. Which is partly why the drinks are free.

Same thing goes for starting down that new professional path. Because when you get too cavalier or overexcited about something, it's easy to forget about responsibilities like paying utilities and calling people on their birthday and walking your dog. Which you'll suffer for, because not everyone can hold it in. (I mean the bill collectors.)

There's always basic "life stuff" to take care of—no matter if you're drunk on a dream, on love, or on Cuervo Gold—and you need to account for all of it when considering how many chips you want to put behind this career thing. Even the one you've

> 66 **To climb steep hills requires a slow pace at first.** 99
>
> —Shakespeare, who was probably making a dirty double entendre

always wanted, more than to see your boss embarrassed in front of the company, and maybe fall down as he's running away. (Go ahead, take a second and picture it. This is a job you wish for even more than *that*.)

Now there's the other, equally bad approach of just taking up space at the table and not really playing the game. Which is different from having the dream and thinking it to death, like we just talked about. No, what I mean here is doing all of the research and cold calling and informational interviewing, and then just deciding that it's too much trouble, too hard. It all seems so big and imposing—except for the paycheck—that you decide to opt-out before you even get started.

Or maybe you even go through with it, to some extent, and don't have the kind of experience or immediate success you anticipated. But to call it quits because of that? People would only make love once if everyone thought like this.

> ❝ Passions unguided are for the most part mere madness. ❞
>
> —Thomas Hobbes, who worried about this sort of thing professionally

Right now in your career, your biggest obstacle isn't an a-hole manager or a boring job or even an anemic social life—it's actually *inertia*. (Learned that in a class known around campus as "Physics for Poets.") Anyway, as far as I gathered from the attention I managed to pay, you've got to overcome inertia to get anything moving;

the bigger the harder. So for something as heavy as your career, inertia's not going to let you have it that easily. Meaning you've got a lot more legwork in front of you, leading to just a handful of leads, most of which probably won't pan out, and cost you a bunch of gas money in the process. And that's a good month.

But if you love it, even after all that—*because* of that—then you obviously can't stop. You just keep shoving and sweating, blister by blister, until you find the right opportunity. Which leads to the next one, which leads to the

> 66 **If we resist our passions, it is more from their weakness than from our strength.** 99
>
> —François de la Rochefoucauld, who resisted signing his full name wherever possible

next, which leads to you paying rent eventually. And then at this point you've got *momentum,* which is just as hard to stop. (Except in Vegas.)

Lie no. 97
Failure Means You're Wrong or Not Good Enough

Estimates are that by your early twenties, you will have heard the word "can't" more than twenty-five thousand times. Primarily from parents, managers, and loan officers.

Unluckily, whereas most things pass unmolested from ear to ear with kids and teenagers, this is one that seems to stick. Maybe because youth is so much about being told what to do—and especially what not to—that it becomes part of our imprint. Or maybe as children we buy into the idea that, because the grown-ups in our life haven't been able to pull it off, it's not possible. Or maybe we just want to keep a running total of all the stuff that's going to give the old man an ulcer.

Whatever the case, it's a message we carry with us

A Grande Stupid

"In the course of the year I spent trying to raise money, I spoke to 242 people," recalls Starbucks Coffee Co. founder Howard Schultz, before we were all buzzed on his French Roast. "And 217 of them said 'no.' Try to imagine how disheartening it can be to hear that many times why your idea is not worth investing in."

Now try to imagine the bruises they've since inflicted upon themselves. And, worse, imagine if Howard had actually listened to these guys. Where would we read and have blind dates?

—From *Pour Your Heart Into It*

right through adulthood, and with mixed results: Sometimes, after failing at a task, the Magic 8-Ball says not to try it again, and it's right. This can include things like drugs, opening up a restaurant, disagreeing with your boss in a meeting, believing she's eighteen, paying retail for jewelry, and backpacking through Europe without one of those little Canadian flags sewn to your bag.

And They Need a Haircut

"We don't like their sound, and guitar music is on the way out."

—Decca Recording Co., rejecting the Beatles in 1962

For most other things, though, getting it wrong the first or second or even third time is just a setback, a yellow light, an opportunity to rethink things and try it again from a different angle. Because people fail all the time—especially successful people. And what differentiates them from everyone else isn't that they're so much smarter or better looking or more talented, as we'll talk about next; they're usually just stubborn as all hell and can't stand to lose.

You know the type, ladies. You'll turn a guy down dozens of times, but never quite shut the door all the way. And damned if he doesn't keep asking you out, again and again, until you finally give in. These are the kinds of people who get what they want in life. Even if the courtship turns out to be more fun than the date.

This very book you're holding, in fact, is a perfect testament to sticking with it—and I get to tell this story because I'm the author, and I've earned it, damn it! I actually got the idea for it back in 2000, and spent the next year getting rejected by thirty-two literary agents (finally got one, but then September 11th happened), which led to passes by twenty-seven publishing houses—more or less everyone who publishes these kinds of books. Or, more accurately, doesn't. Not taking no for an answer, I started my own publishing company, and quickly proceeded to lose upwards of $30,000. Plus the book was shit.

Fast forward to 2004, I have another book idea, get rejected by an astonishing 153 agents, passed on by another 22 publishers, and unexpectedly get a deal to rewrite my first book. So don't talk to me about giving up because you fall-down-go-boom. You fail, you learn, you succeed. Everyone else can bite it.

Lie no. 98
Success Is More Talent Than Hard Work

What's most aggravating, oftentimes, about not being able to pull off what you want is looking at some of the people who have. Crap and rubbish and complete wastes of resources and energy are everywhere in the marketplace. Particularly where Hollywood is involved.

But you've got to give them credit, these hacks. Somehow they were savvy and connected and promiscuous enough to get where they are today, and people seem to have bought into their load. For now, anyway.

But instead of being angry and jealous about it, the smarter move is to get motivated and persistent. Because that's most likely how they got where they are today, being one of God's rush-jobs and all. Without the brains and the looks and the platinum AmEx card, odds are they stayed later,

Rocky Road

The earliest stonecutters must've had nothing better to do, because talk about a tough job: They could sometimes hammer away at a rock a hundred times without even a crack forming. (And keep that in mind when you're bugging your boss for more performance feedback.)

But damned if on the 101st blow, that mineral didn't split right into two. So sometimes you're making progress without being able to see it. And eating dirt in the process.

worked harder, schmoozed more, and generally out-hustled everyone they were up against. Well, that or they were nauseatingly lucky.

And even then it's closer to the way Thomas Jefferson saw luck, saying, "I find that the harder I work, the more I have of it." Which can also be said of eyestrain and weekends by yourself, but the point is that opportunities tend to find you when you're consistently putting yourself out there.

Which may mean going back to school to get the right degree, or taking another grunt job and earning your way back up, or even just hanging out a little longer at your current gig—working on some new initiatives and kissing a little more ass. It's different for everyone, depending where you are, what you want, and who you know. Mostly who you know. Really, almost entirely who you know, so focus especially on the mingling.

It's Not in the Sofa

Except for the lucky and the stupid, keep in mind that fulfillment doesn't just happen.

Unlike "faith, wisdom, and romance" which "sometimes lie in wait for us," as genius humorist P. J. O'Rourke puts it, "Happiness is the TV remote, the car key, the other earring of life."

And P. J. should know: He's traveled to more places and consumed more alcohol than all of us, and is still looking...

Otherwise, there's just no excuse for not going after your happiness, and hard. In a country that's formally in pursuit of the stuff, we really take for granted our freedom to shake the Invisible Hand without being arbitrarily shot, jailed, or starved by our government. (For a small annual fee of 30-plus percent of everything, that is.) Regardless, the only system worse than capitalism is everything else, and you literally have the best chance in the world to make it here.

Again, Hollywood.

Looking at it this way, you've already gotten a bigger break than about *six billion* other people, give or take. Except for your manager, I know.

> 66 **Many of life's failures are people who did not realize how close to success they were when they gave up.** 99

—Thomas Edison, who gave us light, movies, and music by being a hardhead

So we've already decided that your parents might not be Kool and the Gang with your career choice. Unless, of course, you really do want to be a doctor or lawyer or something cliché and lucrative like that. Otherwise, you're probably going to go up against the, "I paid for this education, I get to say how you use it" argument, which is completely unfair and accurate.

Accurate insofar as, yes, they did pay for it—or at least kicked in some cash for books and pizza and stuff. And, sure, they've got a vested interest in seeing you go on to do something that'll cover their retirement community or live-in nurse later on. This is part of the thinking.

The other part, the bigger one, has to do with you having the career or doing the things they never got to, or weren't good enough to do. Half the reason people have kids in the first place is because a Boston terrier doesn't leave much of a

> 66 **To be independent of public opinion is the first formal condition of achieving anything great.** 99
>
> —German philosopher Georg Hegel, who had to say this, being crazy and all

legacy behind. And they can't do a lot of vicarious living or bragging to friends through an animal that runs around snorting and licking itself.

Now that's a pretty heavy burden to be lugging around. Especially when you still need to ask them for money. And it's not like they don't want to see you happy and fulfilled and doing something you genuinely love. It's that they *really* want you to stop asking them for money.

This never stops, though, so you can put that one to bed right now. And as the happy part goes, it's supposed to be *their* version of happy: Money, security, prestige, all the stuff they missed out on, or got a taste of, during the '80s. Which they then used to send you to the right schools, raise you in the right neighborhoods, and buy you the right clothes and toys and friends. Now you're "soft" and "dreamy" from the comforts of your childhood. Which, if I'm not mistaken, is exactly what they set out to provide you with. And this coming from kids who burned their bras and had sit-in war protests and smoked out more than you ever have?

It doesn't help, either, that Gen Y is turning to their parents for guidance and support more than any other in recent memory (now that the twenties are the "new teens"). So, other than calling them hypocrites and asking that they don't postdate the check, how do you deal with it? I say surprise the hell out of the folks and handle the situation exactly as they would: Punish them.

That's right, turn it completely around and make them feel bad, like they haven't done enough to support you. Good parents are constantly paranoid about that sort of thing, and you can really do some solid damage with this. Shout and cry, don't call or visit for a while, really put it to them. And once you do open up again, Mom and Dad will be so hungry for your affection that they'll get on board with just about anything.

Alternatively, you firmly assert yourself as a grown adult, whose decisions and consequences are yours alone to make and bear. Period. Well, that and maybe an offhand remark about how well they get along with their own parents.

Lie no. 100
Irrational Is Impossible

Irrational isn't impossible; irrational is *impractical,* which is a very different thing.

People pull off irrational stuff all the time. Reason usually being that they were around a bunch of other irrational people, who never questioned the intelligence of what they were doing. This is how a lot of companies get started, by the way. Like mine.

Adidas has even gone as far as saying that "Impossible Is Nothing." I personally wouldn't take it that far, but I like the sentiment. It speaks to the fact that as we get older, we come to believe that our dreams are just that— ridiculous, unattainable fantasies. Not that slipping on a pair of their shoes will get you any closer, but it may just get you excited and inspired enough to try it and probably break your leg.

> ### And Then the Agent...
>
> "Every act of progress the world has ever known began first with a dreamer. After him came the scientist or the statesman, the expert or the technician. But first came the dreamer."
>
> —Maurice Davis

But if there were ever a reason to break it, this is the one—going after something you desperately want, and have a relatively low statistical chance of achieving.

Kind of like Brad Delson did.

If you recognize that name from somewhere, I did first; we went to UCLA together. He and I weren't close friends, but it was one of those things where you'd stop and say what's up if you passed one another on the way to class. Anyway, back then he had a humongous white-boy afro—which made him just that much taller than me—and he was almost as smart: Except he insisted on pursuing this whole music thing, whereas I was going to pull in a solid $40K a year in consulting, safe and sound. A couple years later, though, I was already on job number two, verging on number three, whereas Brad was still at number one. On the charts, that is—as the lead guitarist for Linkin Park.

Completely irrational, obviously, but not impossible. At least not for Brad. Still, you've got your own impossible dream out there, with just as bad odds of it happening. And I'm still not saying that you toss everything and run out to go do whatever this is.

I'm just saying that if you've written it off, don't. Not unless you've changed your mind, and haven't had somebody else do it for you.

Because there are plenty of willing applicants: Your parents, for one. Your friends for another. Even society at large, which has about as large of an influence. Seinfeld got famous talking about it, always walking around quipping, "Who *are* these people?"—but then relating it to something dumb, like how socks go missing from the dryer. When you think about it, though, Jerry was asking a better question than we assume.

How many people just sort of roll over from the pressure of the masses, worried about what the neighbors will think, even though they hate them? But then, in a twist, consider who we hear about more often than we'd like to: Not your everyday businesspeople,

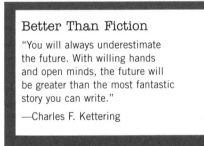

Better Than Fiction

"You will always underestimate the future. With willing hands and open minds, the future will be greater than the most fantastic story you can write."

—Charles F. Kettering

unless they do something really bad and interesting. No, it's characters like Michael Jackson and Dave Chapelle and whatever athlete got arrested or into a fight this week. It's the nonconformists we love. Even though they should really be conforming.

So my final thought to you is go after your passion— irrational, impossible, or otherwise. Don't play it too safe, don't play it too stupid, but make sure you do go play it. That's why they sell condoms and insurance and career books.

Acknowledgments

The person most responsible for this book is, of course, me. Anyone who says otherwise is just kissing ass.

But business is about kissing ass, kids, so let me start with Bethany Brown, my senior editor. And I really mean it, because this whole thing was her idea; I was trying to sell her a book about sex. If anyone asks, then, it was Bethany's brilliance and foresight to recognize my uncommon and staggering potential—and then to push my pub date back to April. But no worries: Her experience and savvy helped to make this so much stronger a book, and I'm thankful she was there to cut everything I shouldn't have been saying.

Next comes Liz Trupin-Pulli—the best-est-est literary agent in the whole wide world—who never stopped trying, even when I was ready to. For all you aspiring young authors out there looking for representation, this woman is unfailingly responsive, on top of everything, and always willing to tell you the truth. Exactly what you'd want in an agent. (Or a lover.)

Business aside, there's my mom, who I lean on to a fault, dearly love, and am so very proud of. She's like the big sister I never wanted as a kid.

Then, naturally, we have my grandparents Joseph and Dolores, who couldn't take better care of me if they tried—and they would—as well as my pop and stepmom, Perry and Anne, whose post-quarterlife crisis relationship I'm grateful for. When I finally get around to visiting.

I'd also get injured, physically, if I didn't thank my inner circle for their help and support with this book. Okay, fine, my only circle. But after more than a decade, I'm still not tired of them, and that's saying something.

It starts, as it usually does, with mi amigo mejor, Raymond Muñoz—and his now-wife Jill, who I'm amazed doesn't slap him more often. Then there's my longest-standing friend (and accountant and lawyer) Roshan Sonthalia, who's still so in love with his own lovely wife, Vrunda, I can't decide if it's that obnoxious or if I'm just jealous. Finally we have Rusty Jenkins (hey man, you need a girl!), and my wonderful PR guru Louise Weston, who I wish the very best with her big Canadian hockey player. Picking an athlete over a writer...it's like high school again.

Finally, I'd like to give a shout-out—had to say it—to my fellow "Genex-ers" for their (mostly) good advice: Uwe "the Hook," Alison "Grimace" Friedman, Joe "Pepe" Ward, Mark "Funky Bunch" McGiffin, Ken Sitz, Lisa Connelly, and Maria and Adam Chester.

I promise to forget all of you when I become famous, and have you thrown off my property.

About the Author

Michael Ball is the founder and CEO of Career Freshman Co., the entry level training authority to the Fortune 1000. A former Big Four consultant and Silicon Valley dot-commer, Ball saw too many smart college recruits doing dumb things—besides their jobs—and devoted his own career to making gruntwork hurt less. Michael holds a degree in psychology and business from UCLA, and lives in Los Angeles. He's also widely regarded as an above-average dancer. Check out www.careerfreshman.com for more.

Index

80/20 rule, 127

A

accountability, 48–49, 87–90, 91–93, 126, 182
Albion, Mark, 246, 255, 259, 36
attention to detail, 80–81, 83–85
attitude, 39–40, 56–58, 62–64, 147, 148, 287

B

bragging, 26, 33, 57–58, 62–64
branding, 116–139; commodity, 118; brand associations,
    139; brand promise, 125–126; brand loyalty, 126;
    differentiation, 119–120, 122–124; familiarity,
    128–130; niche, 131–133; value proposition, 131
burnout, 205–207
business case, 161, 163–165, 175, 178, 184

C

careers, changing, 186–188, 230–232, 233–235, 267–269,
    280–281, 310; choice of, 230–250; direction,
    233–235, 300–302; fulfillment, 236–272; goals,
    233–235, 300–302; ladder, 274–276; money, 242–243,
    252–269, ; passion, 236–238, 239–250, 255–257;
    plan, 300–317; purpose, 242–243; safety, 267–269,
    283–285, 286–288; stress, 303–305; timing of,

300–302, 30–308, 315–317; trial-and-error, 306–311, 318–320

clients, 94, 97–98, 123, 227, 289

college, 10–12, 16–17, 24–26, 60, 72, 101, 105

coworkers, 56–58, 59–61, 62–64, 169–171, 177–179, 292–294

CYA file, 93

D

dating, 142, 144; coworkers, 169–171, 292–294; time for, 217–219; bars, 220–222; online, 223–225

DIGJAM file, 178

downtime, 154–156

E

education, real-life, 109–110, 111–113

ethics, 101–104

executives, 258–260

expectation management, 95 *see also under-promise, over deliver*

expensing, 2, 37, 77, 102, 177

experience, 36–37, 106–107, 109–110

F

failure, 80–82, 83–85, 87–90, 309–311, 318–320

feedback, 19–21, 50–52, 76

first 90 days, 28, 57

flextime, 4, 196

G

graduate school, 14–15, 322

gruntwork, v, 4, 16, 18, 31, 33, 39, 118, 120

H

halo effect, 134

Harvard, 36, 70, 79, 201, 214, 246, 259, 275, 278, 303, 304, 312

honesty, 87–89, 101–104

How They Achieved, 70, 72, 188, 245, 284, 310

I

ideas, 53–55, 157–168

identity, 13–15, 116–124, 128–130, 289–291

initiatives, 157–168

intelligence, 16–18, 33–35, 36–37, 56–58

J

job description, 30–32, 41–43, 142–144, 183–185

K

Kelley, Robert, 37, 143

L

layoffs, 40, 142, 219, 286-288

learning, 105–107, 108–110, 111–113, 192, 267–268, 276, 296–297

Lessons from the Top, 41, 57, 81, 106, 271

M

managers, 46–55, 61, 91–92, 108–109, 143, 151–153, 166,
    186, 189–191, 214–216
MBA, 57, 193, 214, 231, 234, 246, 255
mentors, 31, 65–71, 73–74, 107, 135–136, 177
Midases, 135, 144, 177
mistakes, 83–90, 318–320
money; dreams and, 236–238, 242–243, 245–247,
    255–257; happiness and, 239–241, 252–254,
    248–250; meaning of, 261–263, 264–266;

N

networks, 75–78, 135, 138

O

office politics, 142–171
opinions, 11, 48, 61, 67, 145–147, 150

P

parents, 3, 11, 19, 24, 41, 62, 73, 94, 117, 162, 211, 225,
    243, 257, 300, 301, 310, 312, 318, 324-326, 329
passion, 236–238, 242–243, 245–150, 252–257
paying dues, *see gruntwork*
performance reviews, 20, 60, 80, 91, 180, 182
personal relationships, 169–171, 217–225
priorities, 41–43, 122–124, 131–133, 199–201, 208–210,
    214–216, 226–228, 255–257, 264–266, 289–291
professors, 11, 14, 24, 27, 34, 56
promotions, hard work, 174–176; lateral, 192–194;

momentum, 180–181; new positions, 183–185; recommendations, 177–179

Q
Quarterlife Crisis, 13, 200, 309
quitting, 295–297

R
recruiting, 30–32, 142–144
résumés, 171, 187, 267, 277–279, 295

S
sleep, viii, 17, 43, 46, 109, 111, 119, 169, 200, 203-206, 218, 245, 280
success, vi, viii, x, 18, 62, 117, 122, 155, 173, 181, 185, 201, 202, 219, 245, 252, 255, 257, 258, 278, 303, 304, 316, 320, 321, 323

T
talent, x, 34, 36, 75, 321
teamwork, 59–61
time management, 270–272
training, 31, 34, 103, 113, 160, 179, 190,
transfers, 186–188, 189–191
trial-and-error, 309–311
trust, v, 27, 34, 37, 48, 74, 81, 123, 134, 143, 225, 253, 300

U
under-promise, over-deliver, 94–96, 98

V

values, ix, 6, 188, 236, 237, 260, 266, 290, 293, 306

W

Wal-Mart, 31–32, 34, 40
work – life balance, 196–228

Z

Ziglar, Zig, 94–95